Anna Stockton's Theory of Everything

I0504648

By

Nancy Ferrier

Contents

Dedication

To Art, my partner, and Art - the pursuit of everything beautiful and harmonious.

Chapter 1 – Celebration

Some people have a dream.

Some people have a plan.

Anna Stockton, in her life, seemed to stumble from one unintended consequence to the next.

****

A blast of frigid air delivered an icy shock to her face as she opened the SUV's back door and stepped out from its warmth into the starry night.

"It's colder than a witch's tit. No offense, Rima." Anna zipped up her puffer jacket and pulled the hood over her head as she climbed out of her friend Jo's vehicle. She slammed the car door catching the seat belt, and looked apologetically at Jo, who was rolling her eyes in exasperation. "You do that Every. Single. Time." And turning her exasperation to Rima, "Don't you have some sort of Wiccan spell that you can do to warm things up a bit? It's too early to be so cold."

"Can't interfere with Mother Nature now, can we." Rima said, flashing her elvish grin with her pale green-blue eyes sparkling under a fringe of neon blue bangs. "No offense taken Anna, my tits are jumbo snow cones." she said, rubbing her generous breasts for warmth.

Anna let out a visible puff of breath as she theatrically retracted the seat belt and carefully closed the car door with an apologetic grimace toward Jo. Glancing at the colorful gift bags her friends retrieved from the rear of the car, she smiled, thinking of all the birthdays they had celebrated at the local Olive Garden. They knew the waitresses there and were allowed to linger for hours over their celebratory feast, leaving behind the residue of gift wrappings and bows of their party without sour looks from the servers. As they entered the warmth of the restaurant, a cheery smile from the hostess welcomed the regulars. She guided them to a booth in the back.

The server appeared saying, "Classic cosmos all around tonight ladies?" to a trio chorus of "Yes, PLEASE!".

"So, how is our golden-throated WPLY "Plymouth-Good to Know gal" directed Anna to Jo, who hosted a talk show at the town's radio station, interviewing state politicians, talking up school programs, art projects and making small-town celebrities of local heroes.

"I got into trouble for my mushroom commercial. The producer said it was too sexy." Jo grimaced.

"What's so sexy about canned mushrooms?" asked Rima.

"Mmmmm, Mancini Mushrooms." Jo breathily replied in an exaggerated Marilyn Monroe whisper.

"Thank God it's radio. Imagine getting all hot over a woman in her sixties." Jo added in her pleasantly normal voice.

Anna looked at the attractive blond who could have held her own against any thirty-five-year-old on public media.

"It's all about experience and confidence. Think Diane Sawyer." Anna said with authority.

The server came back with their drinks and the three women who referred to their solid friendship as the "Triumvirate" toasted yet another birthday. Another chance to sigh and reminisce about their younger days when the three would automatically make heads turn upon entering a room. Rima was a petite curvy redhead with an explosion of waves and arresting blue-green eyes, Jo was a statuesque blonde All-American girl, and Anna was the sleek, exotic almond-eyed one with a fall of waist-length shiny dark hair. They would laugh about surviving their misadventures, ask who had looked up a former lover on Facebook, talk about their lives filled with work and family and grandchildren, and bemoan battling with expanding waists and graying hair.

They ordered against their better dietary judgment from the menu roundly criticized by the foodie cognoscenti and yet thoroughly enjoyed by the three old friends. Then the gift bags were presented along with numerous comic and crude cards, making them snort and giggle and some heartfelt notes celebrating their mutual affection.

Anna opened a large package from Jo, stripping off the paper and bows to reveal a handsome red leather designer handbag. Peering inside, Anna found tucked in a pocket a generous gift card for T.J. Maxx. "Shoppiiiing!!!" she squealed.

"Your favorite activity." Jo said, gifting Anna again with her dazzling toothpaste commercial smile.

Rima proffered a small package that Anna guessed was jewelry.

Slowly prying open the box, she glimpsed at the raw pearl drop earrings, the pearls being a teardrop shape and a shade of creamy white, wrapped in rose gold wire and twisted to resemble a flame at the top of the pearl.

"How lovely," Anna said to Rima. "I have never seen pearls like these before."

"They are called flaming pearls, and they represent the search for enlightenment." Rima explained.

"Well, perhaps there is some hope for me with these." Anna said, removing her plain silver hoops and replacing them with the exotic drops. She dangled the pearls with her fingers making them shimmer and glow in the low restaurant light.

"You ladies sure know how to make a seventy-year-old girl feel special." Anna said with great fondness.

Jo gazed with affection at Anna, with her now short brown hair showing streaks of silver at either side of her temples, emphasizing her dark smokey eyes.

"We're all aging. But dammit, we still look good! And I'll cast a very nasty spell on anyone who says not." Rima said.

As the hot plates of pasta were presented, with delicious salad and breadsticks, Anna leaned over the table and, in a low conspiratorial voice, said, "Paul has agreed to give me some creative space in his studio at Western Avenue. A little space where I can paint and collage and let out my creative urges."

Anna attacked her noodles Alfredo, with gusto, twirling the pasta into cheesy globes on her fork.

"I'm obsessed with this idea I came across at work in the science museum. It's this mathematical concept called Phi. It stands for the mathematical sequence that, when you graph it, forms the basis for the spiral. I have the urge to paint things spirally. Flowers, snowflakes, nautilus shells, spiral galaxies. It's called The Golden Mean in art."

There was a moment of silence as Jo and Rima stared incomprehensibly at their friend.

"Well, alrighty then." Jo said. "What makes these spirally things so special?"

"The idea is this lovely math called the Fibonacci Sequence that informs so much of what we perceive as balanced and beautiful. I want people to think about it. That harmony is everywhere and wants to be noticed. That spiral form is even in your DNA."

"Huh," said Rima, "Is this some approach to spirituality? Are you going to be my next guru? I've read some Chopra stuff on that."

"Noooo, it's just MATHEMATICS!" said Anna, perhaps a bit defensively.

"Maybe I could do a radio segment about it once it's developed." said Jo trying to be supportive.

"You two are going to love this. I'm going to make a beautiful mathematical concept fun and easy to understand. The idea is to make public art, supply free stickers for people to tag their lives with. It will be a small message to find beauty everywhere."

"We'll certainly take the free stickers." Jo said.

"I'll keep some in my fairy studio, too." offered Rima.

"It looks like a reading with the guys is in order." Rima added with air punctuation on 'guys'.

"Hmmm, it's been a long time since we engaged in that little talent of yours." Anna said, "Could be interesting."

Anna smiled her Mona Lisa half-smile as the assortment of Italian pastries arrived at the table. She took her ricotta pie covered with dark chocolate icing and laughed as she pointed to the white chocolate swirl that decorated the top of it. "Phi," she said, with a sparkle in her eye.

Chapter 2 – Could It Be Magic

Thoroughly sated with pasta and wine, the Triumvirate tumbled out of the restaurant, laden with gifts, back into Jo's SUV and headed for the Plymouth waterfront, where Rima kept her small fairy studio. This magical place is where Rima created charming tiny houses and other enchanting accoutrements that she sold at fairs and on her website. Upon entering the studio, everywhere the eye scanned, there were wee fairies peeking out of cottages made of twigs and moss decorated with acorns, leaves, and dried flowers. Gnomes were having tea inside a beautiful old clock. Elves were hidden in books and peering out of teapot houses. It was a delight to enter Rima's enchanted world.

She pulled out chairs for Jo and Anna and placed them across from a soft armchair covered in pretty floral fabric, where Rima would sit. She then had Anna and Jo light candles that were placed in various places around the studio. Next, Rima went to a wooden cupboard and took out a ceramic bowl with a stick of twigs made of herbs bound together with twine and smelling of sage and lavender. Rima took a lighter and lit the end of the smudge stick. She then went around the room, lifted it in the air spreading the herbal scent throughout the room. She then approached Jo and Anna and circled their heads and then her own with smoke rings.   Jo and Anna breathed in the spicy aroma of the smoke motioning with their hands to bring the smoke toward them.

As she was performing her cleansing ceremony, Anna thought of how her friend had come to this extraordinary magical way of living. Decades ago, they were young marrieds living by the sea in Manomet, a village outside of Plymouth. Rima was already ensconced in her Cape when Anna moved into the Saltbox next door. They had spied on each other when Anna was moving into her cottage. Bringing cartons upstairs, Anna peered out of her attic window and looked down at a cute redhead stretched out on a chaise in a tiny bikini in her next-door backyard. Anna determined that she could not see being friends with anyone possibly tempting to one's spouse. Rima, in her chaise, glanced up and saw the new slim exotic neighbor with long dark hair and made the same determination. But in time, they beat a path to each other's homes through the spit of woods between their houses and drank gallons of mugs of tea. They would take long walks on the beach while their daughters played together. Jo was Rima's best friend since grade school, and she quickly joined the two, their group forming the Triumverate.

Rima came to Anna's back door one day, looking ashen and nervous. Anna put the kettle on and asked what was bothering Rima, knowing that it probably had to do with the passing of Rima's much-beloved grandmother. Rima said nervously, "I heard from my Gram." Anna looked curiously at Rima. "Whatever do you mean?"

Rima said, "I was just journaling, writing about how much I missed her when suddenly, I started writing something I wasn't thinking. My writing was quick and ahead of what I was thinking. It was like a message from Gram. She said to look for her emerald ring at the bottom of a carved wooden box I took from her house. I looked through all the souvenirs I haven't had the heart to examine yet, and look." On Rima's hand was an antique emerald ring.

Anna said, "Gosh, I've heard of this phenomenon. It's called automatic writing."

Rima said, "I've heard of it too. I was so close to Gram. And we seemed to be mentally linked somehow.
Do you think I have psychic powers?"

"Whoa, tread carefully, my friend." said Anna. "You have no idea what lies down that path."

But treading carefully was not Rima's style. She would gingerly develop her automatic writing, eventually contacting what she would call entities from our world and beyond. They explored this strange world of metaphysics, going to endless lectures from famous psychics and spiritual teachers, always with somewhat of a critical eye and looking out for charlatans. But there remained enough there to understand that "There are more things in heaven and earth that are not dreamt of in your philosophy." as Shakespeare wrote.

Rima ultimately decided to take automatic writing one step further and verbally communicate with her "entities." Her mother, a strict evangelical, was horrified and insisted she was communicating with Satan. But Rima persisted and went public with her abilities. She would give her readings with Anna to make sure that she would return from whatever alternate reality she was visiting when Rima went into a trance.

As they continued with endless classes and spirituality courses, they were instructed to meditate and then draw their spirit guides in one past life regression class. Anna was a bit let down because people were coming up with deceased and beloved relatives, ancient spiritual guides, angels and goddesses. Anna prided herself on being somewhat of an artist, and all she could come up with was a stick figure with a head that looked like an inverted pear and hardly any recognizable features. A couple of years later, she would be sitting in a state of semi-shock in a movie theatre when she watched the end of a movie, Stephen Spielberg's "Close Encounters of the Third Kind".

The scene showed that a spaceship had landed. Astonishingly, a creature emerged from it, looking very much like her stick-figure spirit guide. Anna chalked it up to some synchronicity of forgotten esoteric information surfacing in her mind. Rima had a different view. She believed it was one of her friendly "entities."

But eventually, Anna became disenchanted with the people who wanted her friend to become their guru. She was fascinated with the extraordinary stories that so many people seemed to have within the culture of psychic experiences and talents. But in time, she fell under the spell of science. Anna was amazed at the discoveries that were making their way from academia to the public interest. At least to the extent that a layperson could understand. She had access and information from well-known figures in science, who lectured at the science museum, the bonus she indulged in when she wasn't tediously working over numbers in the accounting office.

Anna still was fascinated by beautiful crystals and gemstones that Rima claimed had energetic powers. She still enjoyed lovely philosophical writings that encouraged compassion and kindness and the curious phenomena surrounding this field of interest. Much like her interest in Catholicism in the old tradition with its gorgeous classical Masses, liturgical music and Renaissance art, regarding the religion of her youth, she just retained a fondness for aesthetics with no firm beliefs.

Belief is such a strange thing, Anna concluded. It can produce miracles, produce anecdotes of synchronicity, and like the famous Scottish gardens of Findhorn, grow fantastic vegetables in the sand with the help of elemental energies like the imps in Rima's enchanted studio. Yet, at the same time, belief can devolve into dangerous religiosity, weighed down by dogma, rituals, and rules, building walls of judgment and isolation against non-believers.

But in Rima's world, all was acceptance and love. She traversed the fascinations of the otherworldly with boldness and creativity. If she rushed in, heart and head, where angels feared to tread, she was the wisest and happiest of fools.

So, after divorces, husbands, and boyfriends gained and abandoned, adventures and misadventures, heartbreaking losses, and extraordinary moments of illumination, they remained through it all - the three old friends and their extraordinary friendship. They were soul sisters who were searching for magical moments.

Rima made herself comfortable in the armchair, smiled, and said, "Bye."

Her breathing became very still, and she announced that her entity had replaced her consciousness by saying, "Good evening," in a slightly altered voice.

Anna said, "Who is speaking?"

From Rima's mouth came a gentle voice saying, "Djagh, who comes to serve you."

Jo, who was always a bit unnerved by this exercise, gulped and asked, "Who are you?"

"I am one who is available to guide the energy of earthly beings.", responded the strange voice.

Anna took a deep breath and said, "Thank you. I am looking to go on a new adventure. Am I on the right path.?"

"You are on the path of destiny, dear one. I will give you two keys to unlock the knowledge you must deliver."

Anna could somehow visualize the strange creature extending long spindles that formed somewhat of a hand to her. The hand held two keys. One an old rusted heavy key, and one just a short thin line of clear, bright energy.

Djargh said, "Observe the ancient key and mentally hold it."

Anna closed her eyes and put out her hand. She could feel the presence of rusted metal, iron, and age in her hand. It was warm. She mentally enclosed her fingers around the key. Her mind flooded with images and sensations. Bitter cold, then the scent of a heavy animal skin warming her, the smell of roasting meat on an open fire, fear of the others, animal skin again, this time an ermine edging the softest velvet in deep forest green, the overwhelming scent of violets in a perfume, fear of the others, searing heat that made the straw of the hut too hot to touch, the trumpeting sounds of an elephant, announcing the approach of the others, the torch lights glistening on the waters of the canal, masked people laughing wildly on the bridge, the scent of spilled wine, lovely music, but fear, looking from the tenement window at the tops of cars traveling on the streets below and thinking from that angle the automobiles looked like cockroaches, afraid of rats, fearful of the others, cerulean silk embroidered with tiny flowers and leaves the green of celery, it is so soft against the skin, but I am afraid the others will choose me. ELO is playing in the background as she sets the table for a family feast. Everything smells delicious, and there is a pecan pie for dessert. She hopes that the guests will behave themselves when the other is seated at the table. It could get so ugly. The headmaster is harsh. Gazing out of the window, I see the others coming to the school. You can hear birdsong. Will you be taken this time? There is always the presence of fear. The others are the danger. Anna felt overwhelmed by disturbing sensations. She could feel her pulse racing and tears forming in her eyes. Jo was protesting, shouting,

"Stop it! Stop! Stop!" It seemed that Djargh removed the key from Anna's hand.

Djargh imparted this mental message, "This only, understand. Fear. Fear of the other. Understand and conquer it."

Anna took a deep breath. Fear. She knew this. There was rational fear that guided caution and self-protection and irrational fear, the thing that caused no end of grief and despair. But that seemed to be programmed into our DNA. So slow to advance and evolve, humanity kept falling over the same stumbling blocks and only occasionally finding the stepping stones.

Jo said, "Are you OK? We don't have to go on with this."

"No, no." Anna said. "It's fine by me if you're alright. Are you alright, Jo?"

Jo glanced at Rima, who sat quite still, with a face calm and devoid of emotion. She was breathing quietly, evenly, waiting to proceed.

"Let's go on." Jo said. Her curiosity about how this would progress conquered any doubts she had.

Anna closed her eyes and could see Djargh's outstretched hand and saw the thin line of energy lift into the air between them. She extended her hand, and the energy key slipped onto the surface of the tip of her index finger. Then, in her mind, she heard the word "Engaged."

She raised her finger. There seemed to appear a stream of dots of sparkling energy, wrapping and permeating everything and everyone in the room. It filled the spaces between objects until everywhere looked like a three-dimensional Seurat painting. It created sparkling energy with things and people defined yet still part of this mass of colorful dots. It seemed to be one whole thing and, at the same time, separate objects with purpose and identity. She was connected yet still was an individual.

Djargh said, "Reflect on what you see here. This concept is the understanding that you wish to impart. The only language that exists to express it is embodied in mathematics. Few speak this language adequately. You are here to create symbols, more comfortable for the earthling to absorb at a subtle level where language fails. If you accept this task, there will be a misunderstanding. Some will try to translate this reality into familiar and misstated terms. Be prepared to persist in offering this message only by your creation."

"I must go. The process will be your teacher, and I will always be watching and guiding you."

This thin clear line disappeared from Anna's finger, and she heard the word "Disengaged."

17

The sparkling dots slowly dissipated like a mist blown away by a warming wind.

Rima moved a bit in her chair. She whispered, "Thank you for your guidance." and put her hands to her face. When she lowered her hands, her pale eyes were shining.

Jo, who had been holding her breath for the last few minutes, blew out a "Phew!" and looked at Anna to see her reaction.

Anna sat with her eyes lowered, trying to decide what she should take in and accept and what may have been just her imagination. There was much to contemplate and attempt to decipher.

"Well, thank you Rima, I think." she said a bit ruefully.

"I might be biting off a bit more than I had in mind."

Rima looked at her and smiling her elf smile, said, "It's all written in the stars. We do our best to follow our destiny."

"Well, the stars had better guide me home. My brain is spinning." Anna said.

Jo, wide-eyed, nervously giggled and said, "This should make for an interesting radio spot."

Chapter 3 – Gallery Z

The glowing yellow light from the large storefront windows of Gallery Z spilled out to the sidewalk, where guests gathered chatting, wine in hand, to escape the crowd within.

Paul's one-man show was a great success. The cheese boards were decimated. The naked grapevines, forlornly decorating scraps of brie and gouda and crumbs of water crackers. The scattered detritus of the reception's half-empty wine bottles and empty burgundy-stained tulip glasses were scattered around the café tables in the back of the gallery. Additional framed photos were mounted there, attractive against the brick walls.

The bulk of Paul's photos were in the stark white main gallery. They showed modern urban landscapes captured in detail with highly saturated colors and clean lines.

Anna noticed several red dots below the photos, indicating that it was a good night for sales. Paul was happily explaining to a guest that the image she was admiring and insisting that Braque must have been the original artist was the red hull of a ship, forming an abstract image he called "Mask."

Anna smiled and exchanged comments with many of the familiar crowd who came out faithfully for these gallery openings, a circle of artists, artisans, musicians, and collectors who enjoyed the Lowell art world's creative cultural atmosphere.

Numerous galleries and trendy restaurants are lining the streets with their glowing gas-lit lamp posts and hanging ropes of electric light bulbs. To walk through this section of the city was a pleasurable blend of food smells, music floating out of bars filled with attractive young people finding each other, and a world of every sort of art offered in the gallery windows.

Many old brick mill buildings had been converted into live/workspace for artists, and Lowell became a well-known hub to find new art outside of the traditional Boston and Cambridge scenes.

Paul's space at Western Avenue Studios was located not far from Gallery Z. It would be full tomorrow, with people he contacted today who were curious to see more of his work and other photographers who admired his style and wanted him to do print work for them.

Anna had run a gallery for a while, showing Paul's work. He had garnered a lot of attention from the local press and even had articles in the Boston Globe and the Manchester Union Leader showcasing his work. But it became impossible to keep up working weekends at a gallery and a full-time job at the science museum, so she reluctantly left. The gallery eventually closed when the owner decided to pursue a mid-life career change in the law.

They took part in a Biennale in Florence, Italy. Paul's display was placed right next to Marina Abramovic, the famous performance artist. She would be showing her odd films of abuse and self-inflicted pain, which, though originally stunning, at the end of ten days, lost their power and became tiresome for all the participating artists whose spaces surrounded her enclosure, perhaps confirming the banality of evil. But Paul and Anna enjoyed seeing all the international contemporary art and trying many of the restaurants in the beautiful city. The plates of pasta with their delicious sauces and Florentine steaks were a far cry from the old familiar Olive Garden back home. They would purchase fresh fruit from the colorful rows of fruits and vegetables in the street markets and take them back to their pensione to feast on them with warm bread and wine. They climbed to the top of the duomo's dome, where Paul took photos of the red tile roofs below. There was an old woman hanging laundry on a line strung across a cement landing jutting out from her rooftop, unconcerned that she was unprotected with no railing at all. When not attending the show as required by the Biennale, they roamed the vast covered market and lusted after leather goods in the street markets.

Anna reflected on that wonderful time as she examined the photos of the ancient buildings, market stalls, and the people they encountered. She smiled, remembering the charming pensione where they stayed. Each morning, the owner would arrive in their room with a pot of espresso with her adorable two-year-old son, bearing a basket of croissants, jam, and a generous assortment of pastries. She was fascinated to see that the boy's mass of thick ochre curls looked exactly like the hair on the David replica that stood in the piazza outside of the Uffizi. But everywhere in Florence - in the markets and the coffee bars, one could see the faces and characters that appeared in centuries-old paintings and sculptures. Genetic material so unfairly bestowed across generations to make a city of handsome people still showing a trace of the aristocracy. She was lost in a fantasy of living in a world of cobbled streets and archways decorated with garlands of wisteria and delicious food aromas coming out of the houses and trattorias.

She was interrupted from her reverie by Paul, who said a bunch of artist friends would stay behind to help clean up Gallery Z a bit and then go on to the local Asian restaurant to hear guitar music, drink, and dance.

Anna was a go-along person who was happy to jump in and join the fun and support Paul in all his artistic ventures. But now and then, she felt that she was just a minor player on his stage. Sometimes there would be two or three openings in one week, and she would get a bit weary of seeing the art that was now familiar to her. Conversations seemed to be a bit repetitive. She looked forward to the shows mounted at the little Whistler House Museum, where Paul frequently showed and had won several awards in juried shows. And the receptions there with the glamorous curator and her handsome husband were always sparkling, and the artwork innovative or traditionally beautifully executed.

Anna wondered what she would do when she left her work friends behind in her as she contemplated retirement. She knew she would make the occasional effort to have lunch with them and get caught up with the museum gossip, but the drive to Boston seemed to get more interminable and more annoying as she aged.

But for now, she would congratulate the owner of Gallery Z and her ever-helpful artist son for doing a fabulous job mounting the show, helping herself to the last eclair, and fixing her lipstick for the next part of the happy and successful evening.

Anna found a small table for two by the window that looked out onto the street and the outdoor café tables at the Asian Bistro. Paul went to the bar to order drinks and chat with the guitarist, who was set up for the evening's gig. The waitress presented the menu with delicious-sounding Asian dishes presented in a modernist style.

Anna smiled and said, "It all looks so delicious, and here's me wishing for old-fashioned egg foo young."

The waitress bent down and whispered, "I can have the chef make some up for you."

"Gosh, that would be wonderful!"

Anna ordered from the menu as well, being in a celebratory mood. Paul came back to the table with martinis, extra dry with extra olives and gave his imprimatur on Anna's menu choices.

Anna relished the somewhat upscale version of egg foo young and, being served, offered her compliments to the chef to the waitress, with plans for a healthy tip.

"What are we doing after this week?" Paul asked.

We're going to the Cape with Audrey and the kids, remember? Audrey wants you to photograph Hollie for her senior yearbook pictures."

Paul thought of the sylphlike Hollie and said, "That's going to be an easy assignment."

Anna pondered on their busy lives and said, "You haven't forgotten offering me some space in your studio, have you?"

"Of course not. Just give me a chance to clear away my mess of frames and matting paper."

Anna felt a little thrill of anticipation and used that energy to pull Paul up to the dance floor and switch around partners with the other artist who were now crowding the floor, happily accepting their compliments for a successful opening.

Chapter 4 – Cape Cod

The waves were softly lapping the soft sands of the shore as Anna pushed her chair a bit further under the striped beach umbrella to escape the sun. Audrey was stretched out on a beach chaise, leafing through a fashion magazine, still exposed to the sun to get maximum tanning benefit. Anna tossed a can of spray tanning lotion to her daughter, saying, "Don't burn. You should be spraying every time you come out of the water."

James, her son-in-law, lay under the umbrella on the other side, with earbuds delivering a baseball game that he watched on his iPod, sipping a cold IPA, commenting in his Southern drawl now and then on the merits of the umpire's calls.

"Yes, Mom." Audrey replied, acting out a teenage whine. "You don't have to remind your all-grown-up daughter."

Audrey put her hand over her sunglasses and looked over to the sea wall protecting the summer cottage she had rented to see Paul taking photos of Hollie for her senior yearbook. "Strike a pose!" he joked as Hollie exaggeratedly made like a supermodel in a filmy cotton sundress.

In the distance, Caroline was stretching forward, her long slim legs in an inverted V, collecting bits of driftwood to start the nightly bonfire, where they would sit enjoying the spectacular Cape Cod sunset, sipping wine and indulging in S'mores. Anna took out her sketchbook and rendered a quick line drawing of her lean, lovely granddaughter.

Audrey and her tall and handsome husband James came back East in the Summer to take a cottage in Sandwich to reconnect with her childhood friends and share some vacation time with her Mom and her stepfather. But the girls were older now, Hollie heading off to college and Caroline, having graduated from the University of Kentucky, about to take her first job as a digital marketer at the local TV station. And family vacations would be less frequent as the girls went on to pursue their lives.

Thinking about her Mom's impending retirement, she made a familiar plea.

"Come to Louisville, Mom. The Winters are milder, the city culture is right up your alley, and frankly, with the girls moving on, this empty-nester needs a new project, settling you in."

"I am thinking about it, my only and favorite child. There is a problem with Paul's studio in Lowell. Right now, he has a lot of gallery shows booked. But I get it. Expenses would be less, with my no longer working. And the big bonus is being close to you and the Southern branch of the family. So, it's not off the table. "

Caroline approached them, throwing down the driftwood on the blanket and stretching her lovely bikini-clad self on a beach towel, leaning against the stone wall that led to the sea.

"Did Mom talk you into moving to Louisville yet? She grinned at her Nana with hope, raising her eyebrows over green eyes sparkling with hopeful anticipation.

"Well, perhaps if I can get some free social media marketing advice from the family expert, I might just consider it." Anna said.

"I have one of the weird and wonderful projects that I need to think about promoting once I get it put together. Perhaps I could bargain some homemade macaroni and cheese for some marketing advice?"

Caroline rolled over on her stomach, crossed her ankles in the air, and, placing her chin in her hands, said, "Run it by me, Nana."

"It's a bit esoteric, but I want to do some free art, giving away stickers that illustrate the spiral form. It's based on a mathematical formula called the Fibonacci Sequence. It's so ubiquitous in forms you find in nature that it's a sort of hidden message for beauty and harmony all around us.

Here, I'll draw the symbol I'm using. Anna quickly drew the lowercase Greek letter phi centered in a box with a quick splash of color rendered with colored pencil and turned it to show Caroline. "I think there are all sorts of applications once I get the sticker thing started. Other artists can use it in their street art, decorative crafts, scrapbooking, or anything they'd like. But that means getting involved with social media. And that's where I am completely lost." she said.

I'm going to try to work out of Paul's studio on Western Avenue, but there's very little space. And I'm not sure the drive to Lowell is worth the trouble.

"Oh, that seems interesting, Nana. When you have the materials completed, let's figure how I can help you out. And I will take you up on that macaroni and cheese. Who knows, maybe the name Anna Stockton will be famous like Banksy or Shepard Fairy!" Caroline smiled and playfully patted her grandmother's leg.

Anna was distracted by a middle-aged man walking along the sea wall and stopped to light a cigarette. He glanced their way maybe a few seconds too long and then looked out to the ocean.

"I certainly hope that cigarette butt doesn't land in the sand." She thought. "And he can just keep his eyes in his head and away from my girls." She was relieved when he sauntered off towards the ocean and kept walking along the shoreline.

"I'm getting too hot." Anna said. "Perhaps I'll find some Cheddar cheese and elbow macaroni. I always keep my promises."

She headed back to the coolness of the cottage to shower and read a bit before she concocted her family's favorite comfort food.

Chapter 5 – Western Avenue Studios

Phillipe Stark Louis IV Phantom chairs. Not original of course, but still pricey for Anna. That was the only indulgence she would allow setting up her studio at Western Avenue. All other furnishings were second-hand or bought from office furnishing overstock sales. At the back of the long narrow studio, she installed a large work table to hold painting supplies, and she added a swivel chair. A soft armless chair that opened to a little futon should she want a little afternoon nap was tucked into a corner. There was the student refrigerator and microwave oven stacked on top of it and a small white cabinet to hold a coffee maker and apothecary jars for tea and sugar tubes. Behind the doors of the cabinet, she stored some pretty vintage dishes to serve cheese and crackers during open studios on the first Saturday of each month. At the front of the studio, she put the clear Lucite chairs and a small gray-painted traditional side table with a drawer to hold notepads and pens. Across from that, a narrow brown chest to hold wine glasses and cleaning supplies. On top, she placed a vase of white silk flowers and her newly printed business cards in a clear holder. An old wooden easel leaned against a wall completing the work area. At the back of the studio, a large multi-paned window flooded the studio with light.

A place to create, think, and write. A room of one's own, a room with a view, even if that view was of the railroad tracks outside the old mill building housing 300 artists, a black box theater, a formal art gallery, and a craft beer brewery. The clouded glass of the 18 panes of the window still allowed for a sunset view. Anna gazed out at the orange-to-pink-to-purple display and imagined the acrylic blends she would have to mix to capture those brilliant shades. Just one month ago, standing in her own studio was the last thing on her mind.

Anna had been helping Paul bring a load of photos he had just removed from an exhibition back to the studio when she passed by this tiny empty studio that appeared out of nowhere across from his space. The large studio across the way had always housed a number of fabric artists. When one of the artists left the group, apparently, the management decided to wall off the end of the large studio space and construct a small narrow separate studio. Anna stopped in front of the door that seemed to appear out of nowhere. She dropped off the photos she was carrying in Paul's studio and went across the way to see the possibilities this unexpected space might present. She paced the length several times, biting her fingernails and telling herself all the reasons why this would be such an impractical thing to do when their income was about to become reduced by their retirement. It made absolutely no sense at all to consider, so she walked back to Paul's studio, determined to put it out of her mind, when somehow what came out of her mouth was, "You know that studio across the way? I don't know what I want to do with it, but I want it."

"You want it? What for?" Paul said, adjusting a black and white photograph of the Lowell Falls he had just finished hanging.

"I don't know. Painting, I guess, or writing. I just think it would be nice to have a larger workspace to do. I don't know, just stuff."

"I didn't know you were serious about painting. I thought you were just going to show some of your photography in my studio."

"Well, I used to paint a long time ago. You know that portrait of Audrey as a child that she has in her entryway that everyone thinks is a Seurat? That's mine. I guess over the years, I just gave away or threw out everything. I didn't have a lot of space in my single-girl apartment after my divorce."

"Oh, that's too bad. I like that painting at Audrey's. I didn't remember that you painted that."

He set his attention on a photo of a bicycle frozen on a back porch and covered with snow, called "Procrastination" one of his most popular images. Should I hang this again?"

"Yes, that sells like crazy. I guess people relate to neglecting your things. So, what do you think about the empty studio?"

"I guess. We are trying to cut down on expenses."

"But you are buying that huge new printer for the business. There won't be any space for the kitchen area."

"That's right. And maybe I can store some overflow there."

"Uhm, no. If I take this space, it must be my own. I'll take the kitchen set up, though, and I'll give you a cup of coffee and the occasional cookie."

Paul laughed and said, "Well, I guess that's settled then. Go ahead and let Marc know you want the studio."

Anna had the broadest smile on her face, but her heart was pounding in her chest.

She went back to the vacant studio and started to pace out the wooden floors.

Doubts again started to creep into her mind,

"What on earth have I just done? I don't really know anything about painting. I will never sell anything. I can't write. Everyone here is so talented. And she thought of

34

Paul, who had exhibited his photographs all over New England, New York, and internationally.

She sank to the floor, crossed her ankles, gazed out the window, and followed the empty wall to the door. She could see the creative mess she would fill the walls with. Drawings, notes, quotations, and pages ripped out of magazines for inspiration. A work in progress on an easel and finished paintings with clear labels with her name beneath the title. And a nice little seating arrangement in the front to welcome people to her studio.

"Oh, what the hell. Go for broke. Probably literally." Then she picked up her cell phone and dialed the manager's number.

She returned to Paul's studio, where he was pouring fresh coffee into two mugs.

"Well, it's done. I called Marc and rented the studio. He's sending the contract." She said with more than a bit of trepidation.

"If the walls could use a new coat of paint. I'll help you with that." Paul said.

"Hmm, and I think I'll paint the outside door and my section of the exterior wall red, sort of a brick red."

"Well then, welcome, neighbor." He enveloped Anna in a bear hug and lightly kissed her, and offered her a mug to clank against his in celebration.

Chapter 6 - Finding the Phi

Anna checked the door to see if the red paint had completely dried. Then she took a ruler and pencil and made dots to guide her placement of the modern, block-styled brushed silver numbers. "512A. That's me." She pressed the numbers on and stood back, smiling, and entered the studio, ready to work.

Alizarin Crimson and Cadmium Red. Cadmium Yellow and Lemon Yellow. Prussian Blue and Cobalt Blue. Mars Black and White. Gesso. With these, Anna could create endless tints with many choices of viscosity. She reached under the table and pulled out one of the twelve-inch squares from the stash of canvases of a variety of sizes stored there, setting up the small table easel to hold the first square canvas.

She chose a big flat brush for the backgrounds, filbert brushes for the flowers, a small flat brush for the snowflake and a Nautilus shell, and a pointed brush for the spiral galaxy and the Phi symbol.

She had the images clear in her mind. So she painted quickly, covering the canvas on one and setting it aside to dry. Then taking another square canvas, filling in the image details against a finished background. By evening, she completed all the square canvases but the Phi symbol.

She started with the panel painted a bright cobalt blue mixed with white to create a sky-blue background against which she had drawn the lower-case version of the Greek letter Phi. The metallic gold paint that she used to fill in her circular drawing that ended with a downward stroke from the top center down through the center bottom of the circle made the symbol glow a bit.

Anna contemplated the finished symbol and was satisfied with her first attempt at self-expression.

There was so much controversy about ϕ. To Anna, it was a mathematical symbol that referenced the Fibonacci Sequence. The numerical sequence progressed by adding together the last two numbers in the sequence. 1-1-3-5-8-13-21-34-55 and endlessly so on. When you graphed it, the graph created the basis for the spiral curve.

It is fascinating that this spiral curve, whose mathematical formula resolves to 0.618... followed by more endless dots and by its elegant math, forms the most extraordinary number of familiar natural things. It is found in sunflowers and many other varieties of flowers, pineapples, snowflakes, Nautilus seashells, tornadoes, swirling storm systems, spiral galaxies on a massive scale, and, on a microscopic scale, the DNA molecule. Artists and architects refer to it as "The Golden Mean" and look to Leonardo Da Vinci's Vitruvian Man as the prime example of balance and harmony in artistic design. Some even think it informs the most harmonious music. It has sprouted theories, both fascinating and fantastical. Anna noticed that on social media lately, there is much religiosity surrounding it, insisting on its being proof of intelligent design theories. Anna was not particularly religious. The love of Renaissance art and sacred music was leftover from her early Catholic education and stayed an essential part of her. And when she had the occasion to visit a church, she loved the lingering scent of incense and the earnestness of many people of faith who frequented their places of worship where they could be reminded of the qualities of compassion and charity. But she thought that dogma was not for her. So she relegated dogma to archaic rules set up for the reasons of civil order and governmental control.

Anna loved the challenges of the 21st century. The chance for humanity to overcome the age-old biological battle of tribalism vs. altruism in human evolution. Richard Dawkins selfish gene vs. E. O. Wilson's insistence on altruism. She came down on the side of the gentle and humble Professor Wilson.

Her project would be to hang her painted Phi symbol in her studio along with her paintings of a flower, a snowflake, a Nautilus shell, and a spiral galaxy. She would make miniature replicas of these into stickers to use for public art. She would invite visitors to her studio to take the stickers for free and use them to "tag" their lives. Every time they noticed the sticker they could remind themselves that they participated in a world with a design for harmony everywhere in their environment and bodies, emphasizing that beauty was ubiquitous. Paul would make prints of the original paintings that she could offer for sale and she had ordered small collector pins with the Phi painting image. She would call her project "Find the Phi." Maybe people could gather in her studio to talk about her take on these concepts.

There was a tapping on the door. The two women she called "Karinda," because they always seemed to be together, appeared at the entrance. Linda ran a studio from which she booked private tea parties, where she dressed in Victorian splendor, with her pretty young assistant dressed as a servant straight out of "Downton Abbey" in a starched white apron and lace cap. They would serve cream teas at those events, offering tiered trays of tiny sandwiches with crusts trimmed, scones with jam, and a delicious assortment of pastries and cookies. Linda also sold vintage jewelry and china and retro handbags for which Anna had a budget-destroying penchant.

Karen maintained the studio right next to Anna's and could often be heard softly humming along to traditional Irish tunes as she painted in oils in her studio. She frequently painted Irish pub scenes and landscapes with slashes of colors in a nearly abstract style. There was a suggestion of unexpected darkness and complexity that made her painting unique. Anna loved to visit her studio and be inspired by her well-developed style.

"Already down to work, I see." Karen said

"Would you like a cup of tea?" offered Linda

"No," Anna replied, holding up her tea-filled mug, "I have some, but I do have some homemade cookies." She pointed the way to the cabinet with a glass cookie jar filled with chocolate chip cookies.

Karinda helped themselves to treats and plopped themselves into the phantom chairs. Anna playfully wheeled her work chair towards them, scooting next to where they were seated.

"I love these Lucite chairs." Linda said.

"I know, "said Anna, "I may never sell a stick of art, but I think I could have already sold those chairs at a profit to almost everybody who's come into the studio."

Karinda got Anna caught up on the mill building gossip, who had a show, sold what, and the availability of an empty studio vacated by a young anime artist next to Karen and across from Linda.

"And I thought I had nabbed the last available studio." Anna said. "But that studio is too big for me anyway. So I'm delighted with my Virginia Wolfish room of my own."

They polished off the last crumbs of the chocolate chip cookie. Then it was back to work for the three ladies. Again, Anna felt a warm appreciation that she had joined a community of friendly and supportive creatives.

She plotted the arrangement of the Phi paintings over the cabinet, where she would replace the white flowers with tall silk sunflowers and square glass containers for the stickers and pins.

Anna collected her dirty brushes, the plastic palette, and her mug into a basket containing detergent and a sponge and walked down the outside hall to the community sink to clean her tools of the trade. First, she pushed the detergent into the base of the brushes and ran them under the running water leaving a rainbow of colors in the oversized paint-splattered sink. Then, she rinsed out her teacup.

It would be two weeks until it would be her first Saturday open studio. She was looking forward to taking her first baby steps into her new life as an artist.

Chapter 7 – On the Radio

"Good Morning, and welcome to Good to Know, Plymouth on WPLY." Jo said, clad in a headset and speaking into a microphone, sitting opposite her nervous friend.

"Today, we are welcoming Anna Stockton to chat about a very intriguing public art project she created in her studio at Western Avenue Studios in Lowell, MA, one of our favorite neighboring cities, where art is alive and thriving.

"Hello, Anna. I should mention that Anna is an old friend who captured my imagination when she recently opened the doors of her studio to me for the first time."

"Hi Jo, I'm pleased to be here."

"Anna, you have an installation in your studio that invites people to participate in, that is called mysteriously "Find the Phi." That got my attention. Can you tell us a bit about it?"

"Well, to begin with, people immediately want to call it "Find the Pie" as though I ran a bakery. And I have to disappoint them by saying there is no apple pie on the window sill." Nor is it Pi, the numerical equation based on the circumference of the circle, which already gets enough attention on March 14th, which celebrates its existence. Also, Pi is celebrated with actual tasty pies.

Jo chuckled, saying, "I was just a little cast down, expecting dessert when I visited."

Anna chuckled and continued, "The installation displays four square panels that have images of a Nautilus shell, a snowflake, a chrysanthemum, and a suggestion of a spiral galaxy. The last image is of the Greek letter Phi used by mathematicians to indicate the use of a weird string of numbers called the Fibonacci Sequence, which adds the previous two numbers in the series to create the following number in the sequence. When you graph that sequence, it forms the groundwork for a spiral. And the spiral form is found in the images in the other paintings. I painted the Phi symbol against a sky-blue background with the lower-case Phi painted in metallic gold, a ring drawn with a stroke from the top of the circle straight down through the middle of the ring. I used the lower-case version of the Greek letter because I thought it was a gentler image than the rigid capital Phi used by mathematicians.

Jo grinned and said, "I think we are getting heavily into the weeds here. Can you explain how all of this math translates into a public art project?"

"Sure'" Anna said. "What it boils down to is this. The paintings are copied onto small removable stickers

43

provided free of charge to people who would like to participate in the project. I provide them with a sheet of instructions on how to "tag" their lives. The instructions suggest ways to use the stickers either as street art or maybe to place them on your car dashboard or refrigerators like a magnet or a mirror in your bathroom. When your eye catches the image, it should remind you of the spiral form that you see everywhere and even exists in your body as the DNA molecule spiral. They may stop for a few seconds and remind themselves that this formula for beauty and harmony exists naturally. Whatever is going on in the world, they encourage us to turn our thoughts to recognize this beauty and harmony.

"That's a beautiful thought. How do my listeners get their stickers and find out more about participation?"

"They can visit my studio at Western Avenue Studios, Studio number 512A, on Open Studios the first Saturday of each month or email me at info@findthephi.com."

"How do you finance this generous sticker giveaway?" asked Jo.

"I have prints on sale of the painting images, have a little collector button of the Phi sign, and accept donations to cover costs. At this point, it isn't that expensive."

"If you have questions about Find the Phi, please get in touch with Anna Stockton. Her contact information is also available on our station's website GoodToKnowPlymouth.com along with pictures of the stickers."

"Thanks, Anna, for joining us today and making our lives a little bit brighter."

"Thank you for having me." Anna said, relieved to have the interview over.

"And now, after a short break, we will move on to the debate over cutting after-school programs."

Jo turned off the microphones and gave Anna a thumbs-up sign.

Anna said, "I was so nervous. Did I sound stupid?"

"Not at all!" said Jo. "Hopefully, you will get some attention from my listeners."

Jo gave Anna a quick hug and looked through the glass window to the green room and motioned to a group of aldermen seated there to come into the studio.

Anna left the radio station thinking, "That didn't go too badly." And starting the car thought... "Next problem, dealing with the paparazzi. There will be paparazzi, right?"

Chapter 8 – Montreal

A quick getaway to Montreal seemed to be in order. Paul had mounted a number of shows, they had consumed copious amounts of cheese and wine at opening receptions, and Anna did her best at promoting his exhibits on social media sending out traditional press releases as well, which resulted in an excellent article in the Lowell Times with an extensive interview. But they needed a break—a change of scenery.

The three-hour drive along Vermont's winding roads through the jagged mountains was as beautiful as the vacation guides promise. They stopped at Moody's in Maine for freshly roasted turkey sandwiches, and the best pie in New England made with tiny Maine blueberries. Paul did not stop along the way to photograph the spectacular scenery, as he usually would, leaving his camera in the car's trunk. This trip would be for relaxing – no photography. Anna made only one stop at an antique shop and bought a vintage 50s necklace of enameled white apple blossoms with matching clip earrings.

When they arrived in Montreal, they left the car in a parking garage, determined to use the Metro, planning to do some shopping in the enormous underground mall, and enjoy walking around Paul's favorite city that he called his home away from home. They stayed at a B & B in the city center, not far from the Metro. Once underground, they picked up some groceries, a baguette, a good size packet of country pate, some grapes, a couple of bottles of wine, and mouthwatering Napoleon pastries to have a picnic on the hotel bed when they had the urge to snack. They settled into the hotel room, with nothing much to put away since this was just an extended weekend stay, and stashed their picnic goodies in the refrigerator. They took the Metro to Place des' Arts and stopped at the stylish Metro bar to have martinis and nibble on freshly made spiral fries. Anna dangled a fry in the air joking about their DNA shape and how she couldn't get away from spirals. Paul stopped in Archambouds to see what jazz CDs they had to offer, while Anna had discovered that she had left her sunglasses in their room and went to the mall to peruse a table of designer knock-off sunglasses. She put on a trendy pair with heavy white square frames. A smartly dressed clerk approached her, waving her finger, saying, "Non, non, non Madame, those are not for you. Try these, it's a better shape for your face." Anna did as she was told and discovered that a slightly smaller tortoiseshell pair was much more suitable. French girls have that je ne sais quoi about fashion, c'est vrai, she thought as she handed over her $10 Canadian. They were leaving the underground, with Anna halting their progress by stopping now and then ruffling through the racks laden with goods on sale placed outside the boutiques. She stepped outside to the open sun-splashed boulevard, putting on her stylish sunglasses. They bought take-out coffees and headed for the fountains spread over a large section of the city, popping up from the streets, making fountain art with music and lights as people walked through the display, trying to avoid getting wet. As the twilight fell, they watched a young woman approach the extensive circular collection of fountains as they went from tall streams of colored water framed by a sunset sky to just bubbling above the pavement, shooting up high in the air, the water dancing to the music. As the giggling girl teased the water with her foot, her friends dared her to go for it. She started laughing and just jumped in, dancing maniacally among the colorful shooting shafts of water. Bending with outstretched arms feeling the water now bubbling at her waist height, she turned around and around, then finally hopped back to her friends as that segment of the fountain display ended.

"How wonderful to be that carelessly young and free-spirited." Anna said, but with maternal instincts coming to the fore, "I do hope she has some way of drying off. She'll catch her death."

Paul said, "That was wonderful. It was all I could do not to jump in and join her."

"What now, my love?" said Anna drinking the dregs of her coffee.

How about finding a club, some jazz, having a drink, and calling it an early night?

"Sounds like a plan." Anna said.

They wandered a bit and settled on a club with a good mix of customers not overloaded with kids half their age.

Finding seats at the bar and ordering drinks, they had a view of the stage where one act was leaving, and the other appeared for their set. It was a Scottish band, three girls playing bass guitar, electric cello, and electric oboe, backed by guys on drums and keyboard. They started playing their style of alternative rock, and half-listening as she conversed with Paul, Anna began to realize that, for one thing, this group that called themselves the Moulettes was very entertaining. Furthermore, they seemed to be singing about biological forms. Anna stopped Paul from talking and said, "Listen. Rockers singing about science?" Anna wondered about the inspiration that guided this unusual band to pick these themes as the instruments wailed. Then, as the band prepared to take a break, the lead singer stepped forward and said, "We're going to take a short break, and we will leave you with this song called 'Patterns.' It's about the Fibonacci Sequence." Then she stepped back and sang her song about Phi as Anna looked wide-eyed at Paul, who laughed and gave her a high five.

They approached the band as they left the stage for their break to buy a CD and chatted with the lead singer, who suggested taking a picture together with Anna's phone. And as she turned to join the rest of the band, she said, with her charming Scottish accent, "Yeah, everything seems to be imbued with patterns and synchronicity, isn't it so?"

Anna grinned at Paul, saying, "I guess I AM on to something. Who knew?" Then they walked out into the night air, musing about music and synchronicity and wondering if they really should go for some late-night poutine.

Chapter 9 – 1st Open Studio

Anna balanced a plate piled high with pecan tarts in one hand and the keys to Paul's studio in the other. Fiddling awkwardly with the tricky lock, she put the treats on the table, fitting it in along with a guest book with a jar of pens, order forms, business cards, and scrapbooks with Paul's press and magazine articles. Paul preferred sweets to the cheese and crackers and fruit or vegetable trays served at most other studios, and the trick was to have him not eat all the offerings meant for visitors.

Last night they had cleared the studio of discarded matting pieces and takeout food bags and cleared the two tufted, crimson velvet benches of rejected prints and odd framing pieces.

She crossed the freshly swept wooden floor to the window and raised the shade to let in a burst of sunlight, illuminating the photographs lining the white walls. She turned to see if anything needed one last swipe of Windex on the glass, looking approvingly at the collection Paul had chosen to display for open studios from his vast inventory of images produced in thirty years of photographic work. There were abstract architectural details that people often thought were paintings, close shots of wildflowers found in an abandoned glass-filled lot located in nearby Salisbury Beach, stark black and white photos of Lowell, Paul's beloved hometown, showing the mill waterfalls, historic houses, and a 1950s-style gas station and shots of Western Avenue Studios itself, a five-story once abandoned mill with a clock tower looming against a twilight sky. These Lowell images always sold well to the townies who enthusiastically supported the artists of Western Avenue.

Peering around to see if there was any need for any last-minute straightening, Anna was satisfied that everything was in good order. She turned to leave when Paul appeared at the door, arriving after parking the car in an off-site lot at the nearby middle school. They had to leave the parking spaces at Western Avenue for what they hoped would be hundreds of visitors ready to enjoy and purchase local art.

Paul grabbed a couple of pecan tarts and, munching them, looked around the studio approvingly. He offered a pecan-flavored kiss and thanked Anna for helping to organize it. Then, entering the curtained-off work area with his large printer, work table, and camera equipment, he took a seat at his desk and turned on the computer. He read the responses to his invitation to this Saturday's event and gave a thumbs-up to Anna.

"Lots of people are saying they will stop by. It should be a good day."

"Terrific!" Anna said, grabbing a tart as she left to attend to her studio for her first public event.

She had filled the walls of her studio with various canvases, all of them painted with different white flowers. Then, finally, she put the fat glass vase of creamy flowers that had inspired the paintings on the table between the phantom chairs.

She inspected the Phi installation she had created and placed over the chest and wondered how people would react. She had ordered little collector pins with the phi symbol and created stickers for a giveaway from the images of the paintings. These she put into small square glass vases and in a much larger rectangular version of the vases placed tall silk sunflowers and dropped two spiral-shaped ammonite shells into the bottom vase. One last container held folded copies of instructions she had written to guide participants in her public art project.

How to Find the Phi

1. Select a sticker (these are removable).

2. Attach it to a familiar place, like a refrigerator, bathroom mirror, car dashboard, lunchbox, etc.……..

3. When you see your sticker each day, remind yourself of the spiral form, such as those found in seashells, flowers, snowflakes, or massive galaxies in deep space.

4. Take moments during the day to notice if there is a spiral form in your surroundings.

5. Remind yourself each time you observe a spiral form that this elegant design is deep within you in your body's DNA. No matter who you are, what strata of society you inhabit, what abilities or disabilities you exhibit, or how you are perceived, you share this very same exquisite design with all of creation.

6. Have fun Finding the Phi!

Find the Phi Stickers

Find the Phi

Find the Phi

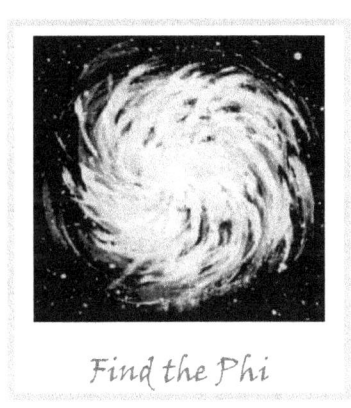

Find the Phi

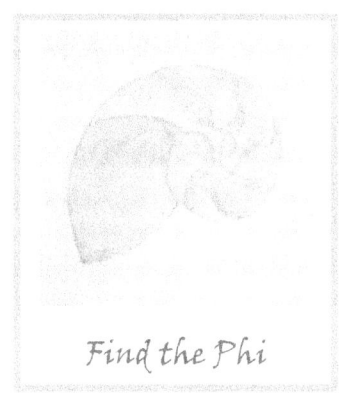

Find the Phi

Find the Phi

Find the Phi

Anna's final touch was to place an open jar containing little packages of multi-colored gummy bears out for the kids and offered coffee and tea to the adult guests.

She walked down the hall stopping at Karen's studio to say a quick "Hi," and complimented her on the painting she was working on, this being a working artist event. Anna then went on to Linda's tearoom to see if she could coax her to part with one of her petit fours. She entered and saw the Victorian lady bent over a chest filling it with vintage evening bags.

"Hi Anna." Linda said, "Help yourself to sandwiches and such."

"I'm afraid I'm going to help myself to that pearl-encrusted evening bag." said Anna.

"And maybe a petit four or a current scone."

"That one is yours, but look at this!" Suzanne said, holding up a shiny hot pink vintage Jessica Clintock bag."

"Don't tempt me. But hold the pearl one for me. I'll pick it up at the end of the day."

"Good luck today, Anna. You must be excited to have your first formal event."

"Excited and frankly frightened of absolute rejection of everything I have to display."

"Oh, they will love it all." Linda said, coming over to give Anna a reassuring hug.

Anna gave a weak smile, took one delicate pastry from the silver tray, and returned to 512A.

Walking to the back of the studio, she looked out of the window. "Breathe." she silently commanded herself, staring at the railway tracks below and visitors starting to line up at the food truck selling coffee and sandwiches below.

She sensed movement behind her and was startled to see a man standing in front of the Phi Project display.

She pasted a smile on her face despite the man's movement to reach inside a pocket for a packet of cigarettes.

"I'm so sorry, but this is a non-smoking building environment. But we have cookies as an alternative." She said with the best attempt at lightheartedness.

She offered the plate, to which the man raised his hand to reject the temptation and put the cigarettes back into his pocket.

Without speaking, he turned back to contemplating the display.

"I'm Anna Stockton," Anna said, offering a handshake, "And you?"

The man quickly shook Anna's hand, saying, "Rick. Rick Berman." Then he turned back to a studied examination of the painting before him.

"Have we met?" Anna blurted out, sensing an odd vague familiarity while examining his profile.

Rick Berman turned towards Anna, staring disconcertingly into her face.

"Interesting little project you have here." he said, in a tone that Anna found just a bit condescending.

She cleared her throat as she looked boldly back at his unsettling gaze.

As she reached for the stickers and instructions to give to her visitor, thoughts of her granddaughters laughing under the sun on the warm sands of Cape Cod popped into her mind.

Startled at the random connection, she envisioned a man stamping out a cigarette in the sand with an unwelcome stare toward Caroline. Or was it past Caroline to the drawing in her hand? A nascent sketch that now was a finished painting on the wall of her studio.

Anna tried to suppress a little gasp of recognition.

She recited her practiced presentation speech for guests, all the while her brain buzzing with contradictions.

Rick Berman let her finish, politely listening, even feigning interest. Then there was a small uncomfortable moment of silence.

"Questions, comments?" Anna said, trying to fill the void.

"How do you know about this symbol?" He finally asked.

"I worked in a science and mathematics environment for many years," Anna explained. The Phi symbol and the Fibonacci Sequence always fascinated me with its pattern of balance, harmony, and its creative implications."

"What exactly do you suppose it implies?" he said.

Anna thought, "I'd better prepare myself for this sort of challenging conversation. People who somehow feel I am somehow appropriating inappropriately a strictly mathematical symbol."

"Just harmony. Are you a mathematician?" Anna continued.

"Yes, you might say that. And how do you propose to use this harmonic information?"

"Harmonic information? Anna could feel herself reddening with consternation clearly showing on her face.

"It's just an image—a symbol for people to contemplate and be inspired by."

Rick reached into the jar of pins and turned it over in his hands.

She was relieved to see the appearance of the faces of her friends, Jo and Rima, at the red door.

Rima immediately caught the look of discomfort on Anna's face and raised her eyebrows in silent inquiry.

Anna smiled broadly and said, "Welcome ladies to my studio!" with a theatrical gesture.

Rick glanced at her friends and back to Anna.

"I'll come back sometime to finish this fascinating conversation." he said.

"Thank you for visiting my studio, and please do come again." Anna said with not an ounce of sincerity.

He took a dollar from his wallet and dropped it into the jar of pins. Brushing past Anna's friends as he left the studio.

Jo said, "Do you know that, man?"

"Weird vibe." Rima said, heading straight for the jar of gummy bears.

"Weird, indeed, Rima." Anna agreed. "I think I had a brief encounter with him on Cape Cod."

"Do tell." Jo said.

"No, not important." Anna said, determined not to let it spoil her opening day.

"Let me invite you into my garden of white flowers!" She said grandly, twirling around the floral section.

Her friends oohed and ahhed, making comments about the subtlety of tone and romantic imagery.

They stepped in front of the Phi display.

"And this is the big project!" Jo said

Rima read through the instructions and fingered the free stickers.

"This is really cool!" she said.

Anna pulled two pins from the glass jar and pocketed the dollar left by Rick Berman.

"My gift to the Triumverate." she said, passing the pins to her friends.

"Our very own cult!" Rima teased.

But an uncomfortable shiver went down Anna's spine even as she laughed." So let's pop over to Paul's studio. He's got pecan tarts."

And throwing her arms around her friend's shoulders, she crossed the hall, guiding them to Paul's studio.

Chapter 10 – Nora

"Am I intruding?"

A tall, thin woman with wiry grey curls stood, framed by the studio entrance, flashing a broad smile.

Anna was delighted with a successful first open studio. The next day she returned to it feeling triumphant. Kicking off her short boots, she switched to her paint-splattered studio mules and covered her sweater with her painting smock. She had just started measuring out some acrylic paint onto a small plastic palette when this unexpected guest made her appearance.

"Not at all. Please come in!" Anna replied, welcoming her with a wave of her arm."

"I'm Anna." She said, extending her hand.

"Nora. Nora Fletcher."

Nora pumped Anna's hand in an enthusiastic handshake.

"I was here at open studios," she said, "but it was so busy that I could barely see anything in your studio."

Anna smiled and said, "It did get very crowded at times."

"But, thank you for returning!"

"Is there anything in particular that caught your eye?"

Nora stepped in front of the Phi project display and widened her clear hazel eyes as she contemplated it for a few silent seconds."

"This." she said.

"It's science-inspired art." Anna replied, chuckling a bit at her inability to come up with a good description.

She pulled out one of the instruction sheets and some free stickers, handing them to Nora.

"Would you like some tea or coffee?"

"Tea, please. Nora smiled.

Anna motioned her to a chair, where Nora settled herself comfortably while she read the paper in her hands.

"Ponder a bit while I make tea," Anna said, "and let me know if you have any questions."

Anna heated the water kettle and prepared two mugs of tea, offering milk and sugar to Nora.

"Just a little milk, please." Nora said, engrossed in the examination of the stickers and instruction sheet.

"This is such a fascinating project." she said, "I've always been interested in math and physics, but this has a spiritual element to it, doesn't it?"

Anna hesitated a bit before she responded.

"Well, that wasn't my intention, I just wanted the observer to look for this wonderful mathematical equation in their surroundings and find the beauty inherent in natural things."

Nora looked slightly disappointed.

Nora offered a bit of balm. "I do understand though, that people are likely to interpret the symbol according to their philosophical beliefs."

"Still, it is there." Nora said.

Anna did not wish to dissuade a probable client, thinking that every artwork proffered was subject to the observer's interpretation.

Determined to make some progress with painting, Anna encouraged Nora to visit again, clearing the tea things.

Nora was delighted with the invitation.

"Perhaps I'll bring along some friends to soak up the spiritual vibes." Nora said half-jokingly.

"I will certainly welcome them" Anna said with great emphasis.

Nora left with one final wave of her hand. Anna turned to her worktable to see the paint had dried on the plastic palette. So, she cleaned it in the common sinks, contemplating the conversation she had had with Nora.

She tried to draw a bit, rejecting one attempt after another, distracted by the afternoon's events. Finally, she tossed paper and pencil aside and decided to pull out the red latex wall paint and repair the scratches on the entrance door made by the visitors to open studios.

She wondered if she should nip this tendency in the bud. The tendency to see her simple street art project as something other than what it was.

Nora was as good as her word. She did sometimes return with a friend or two, sometimes alone when she and Anna would sit with tea, nibbling at cookies and chatting. Slowly Nora revealed her story. Anna had detected a slightly aristocratic Northeast accent when Nora spoke.

She was from a family steeped in generations of "old money."

Her family members were accomplished and well-known. But Nora was the dreamer, the romantic one. She liked to play the piano, especially Chopin.

Nora immersed herself in the arts in quiet defiance of her family's conservative values. She never finished college, thinking it unnecessary. She had no burning ambitions and a small trust fund. Eventually, her family gave up on her becoming a productive member of society and allowed her to live in one of the many family residences, a crumbling Victorian cottage far removed from their busy lives. She would give piano lessons and invite her friends for an occasional visit but mostly lived a quiet and content existence.

Anna conjured up an image of Nora, a naturally elegant woman with aristocratic features and bearing, playing a baby grand piano in an empty room with the sound echoing off the walls with faded floral wallpaper.

Often Nora brought along her eccentric friends. They would plunge into discussions about the Phi project. Anna was fascinated with what they had to say, even wondering if she had somehow missed the point after listening to them. At first, there would be three or four men and women accompanying Nora. Sometimes, she would have to borrow chairs and benches from Paul's studio to accommodate ten or twelve guests who were curious about the Fibonacci Sequence and the thought behind the Phi project.

Anna tried to make it clear that she was not an expert, just a science fangirl.

While she was happy to encourage stimulating discussion, Anna started to wonder if this was taking on an unintended life of its own, well past her intention of piquing interest in a natural phenomenon. And she was frankly flattered by the attention and appreciation. She decided to sit back and enjoy watching this evolve, with Nora lending support in organizing these little get-togethers. Anna added T-shirts with the phi symbol she had created. She set up cubbies to hold different sizes and set up the bowl of pins she still sold for one dollar, though she often gave away more pins than she sold. She even received some donations from kind fans of her project to keep her studio going and cover the expenses of the Phi project.

She was grateful to Nora, who interjected in conversations with her take on the project's symbolism. Anna buried any discomfort she was feeling about misinterpretations, basking in the pleasure of her success. Because, all in all, it was such a small thing. No harm in it at all. Everyone was enjoying themselves.

Chapter 11 – Anna Stockton's Theory of Everything

Anna left the accounting office a bit early, taking the elevator down to the second floor where the lecture was being held. She climbed the Cahners auditorium stairs, the Moulettes "Patterns," still sounding their earworm in her head.

"Ever feel like there's a secret that is close at hand?

And if you could touch it,

If you could reach it, you could peel it back.

It's never quite as it seems…

Numbers, the patterns that move in numbers."

She went all the way to the back row, waving to Jeff, who was working the auditorium lights, thinking that this lecture would be packed with MIT students. She knew that the physicist speakers, unknown to her, would-be rock stars to most of the intelligentsia attendees. She was looking for a quick getaway through the back exit to get to the garage before the mass exit caused a traffic jam.

The auditorium was now filled. As Anna expected, there was a fair representation of MIT sweatshirt wearing students there. The lights went down, and six physicists of varying ages took their places in a half-circle of seats on the stage with a moderator seated in the center—brilliant minds in search of the Theory of Everything. Don't we all have a Theory of Everything, she thought. We decide that this is so, and that is the truth. We have it on the best authority, whomever we determine that source is. Give me a statistic, and I can find someone to counter your argument with another set of statistics or some convincing anecdotal information. Who has the most compelling solution to life's problems? The religious, the skeptics, or these brilliant men and women who look into the heart of matter? And yet, we are all constrained by what we decide is true. We don't know what we don't know.

The speakers began their discussion and slowly led the audience into a foreign, exotic, strangely beautiful universe. They would even admit that the universe was weird beyond not only what we imagine but what we are capable of imagining, as Max Planck said. The common denominator between gigantic spiral galaxies - our earth home existing in only one, not a terribly significant one, among innumerable others inhabiting a universe beyond our capability to grasp in everyday terms, and a micro-universe where matter becomes insubstantial and incomprehensibly seems to come to existence by observation of a potential piece of information rooted in what? Consciousness? And what or who is truly the observer? The religious person would jump to the conclusion that it must be God. The philosopher would wonder if God was Consciousness. The scientist would find a workable idea that consciousness is information in potentialities, perhaps a minute physical property of the brain. To Anna, there was a certain amount of human hubris that consciousness is rooted in human stuff. Did not consciousness exist millions of eons before human beings were a twinkle in creation's eye?

Anna had this notion that pre-Big Bang, there was just this imperceptible shiver, the tiniest hiccup of movement in the field called consciousness. And therein began time, matter, creation, and the universe. The quantum field of endless probabilities connecting and reflecting information. This endless opera of life with themes that repeat and repeat and repeat. Changing forms, evolving but always obeying only the rules of mathematics, beyond language, beyond conceptualizing, beyond random acts of creation. Cosmic information constrained by DNA, history, and circumstances. It is a wildly uneducated guess, Anna knows, but it works for her.

To Anna, it was her Theory of Everything. It explained why people believe as they do, where creative inspiration comes from, synchronicity, illumination, paranormal experiences, voodoo, and miracles. It explains the chicken or the egg quandary of how the brain functions, neurons firing creating feelings, or do feelings fire the neurons. Things are such because we say so. We're making it up as we go along. Anna was quite sure that those present would tell her that a little information was dangerous. But that was her narrative, and she was sticking to it.

After all, to Anna, language would always fail as long as everybody had their own narrative in various languages where things were forever lost in translation. She liked her symbols. The rabbit meant fecundity in Renaissance paintings. Phi is the spiral found endlessly in natural and human-made creations, creating one beautiful thing after another. The famous neurologist Giorgio Tononi ended his book called "Phi" with a symbol that nobody understands, an invitation to creative interpretation. The Italians have got it right. In all things, "bella forma." You see it in their architecture, ancient and modern, their clothing, their food and how it is presented, the opera, la dolce vita. The worst sin is "bruta forma," ugliness.

In mathematical terms, one would always look for harmony and beauty. One would find the Phi.

The brilliant minds onstage are talking of quarks and qualia. The MIT students are asking questions in language that Anna doesn't understand. She wonders if she should pick up takeout on the way home or just throw together a salad. She is in a room full of people resolving the eternal questions of the universe, and her brain is attuned to the rumbling of her stomach. How does a plebe like herself function in a world of information that the average person never even encounters, never mind understands? Ideas that will tomorrow or the next day after tomorrow will have a direct impact on their lives.

We'll all have to learn to adapt, Anna guessed. Or maybe, as the Transcendental Meditation practitioners believe, perhaps information reaches critical mass, then light dawns on the general population. Or maybe the powers in charge will spike the water with something that will make us all just docile happy minions who don't really give a damn.

Anna's brain was spinning, and she was hungry. The lights went up, and she made a beeline for the backdoor to beat the crowd to the garage while people were swamping the stage to shake hands with the information gods of the universe.

Chapter 12 – The Last Day

Anna parked her car at the open top floor of the Museum of Science garage to appreciate for one last time the early morning view of the old Longfellow Bridge with its Salt & Pepper towers, spanning the Charles River reflecting the pale yellow and pink sunrise. Then, turning in the opposite direction, she gazed at the modern cable-stayed Zakim Bridge, its towers mirroring the Bunker Hill Monument obelisk in the distance, then she swiveled again to face the great white dome of the planetarium admiring the jagged mix of modernity and classic architecture that was the skyline of Boston.

"This, I will definitely miss." She thought. Anna was given a lifetime membership to the museum as a retirement gift, and she would come back often. Still, she was sure that future visits would be planned around the pleasures of sleeping late, missing the delight of the rooftop sunrise.

Taking the stairs from the fifth floor, rather than the elevator, to get in a bit of exercise, she approached the long concourse with its brightly colored lines guiding visitors to the correct ticket station- red for members, yellow for ticket holders, green for all other visitors. On the right, she saw the new bank of automatic ticket machines for online ticket buyers. She wondered if, eventually, human interaction would be unnecessary to conduct the business of entry.

Things have been changing since she started working here 22 years ago. The floor-to-ceiling windows afforded a view of the rock garden with its enormous chunk of rose quartz. A seemingly endless line of yellow school buses was parked in front of the museum. Hundreds of school children lined up, their crayon-colored T-shirts defining which school brought them here.

She flashed her ID badge at the entry and headed down to the red wing to get a large Starbucks coffee and say goodbye to the friendly morning staff who always tempted her with lemon pound cake or a chocolate croissant. She chatted with Nancy, the attractive Latina woman who wished Anna well and said she would be missed. After sipping her latte, Anna looked at the Charles River view from the cafeteria's ceiling to floor length windows and thought of the many days she would grab a hot dog for lunch, escape her cubicle's confines in the finance department, and go outside to the Pavilion behind the museum. She would sit on a bench enjoying the sun glittering on the no longer "dirty waters" and watch the Duck Boats go by, full of tourists clacking their yellow quackers and waving to passing boats.

She rode the "'Silver Bullet", ironically named by staff because it seemed to be the slowest elevator on earth, to the administrative offices, thinking about how many times

74

those magical doors would slide open to reveal visiting dignitaries from all over the world. The late Senator Ted Kennedy had been a big supporter and would often make an appearance on the other side of the doors, and the current Mayor of the city and state officials. Famous scientists came here to lecture and receive awards for their work - astronauts, movie stars, George Lucas and Wolfgang Puck, who cooked for the event honoring the Star Wars exhibit. Anna's favorite apparition was when the steel doors slowly opened to reveal Darth Vador and the Storm Troopers, who, in contrast to their reputed evil natures, agreed to take a selfie with her.

Anna encountered various staff members and the president's assistant, who offered congratulations laced with a bit of retirement envy on her way to the accounting offices. The only thing left in her small cubicle was a framed honeymoon photograph of the little café in Quebec City where she and Paul loved to go for almond cream-filled croissants and steaming bowls of cappuccino. And another small photo of her daughter, Audrey, tanned and smiling, posing on the beach along with James, her husband, and Anna's granddaughters, Caroline and Hollie, looking like Botticelli goddesses in their fluttering summer dresses, hair blowing in a summer breeze.

It was early, so the other cubicles were not yet filled with sleep-deprived accountants. Hearing Anna rumbling around her desk, Mila, with her lovely Russian accent, and Phil, the statistics pro, came out to say what fun the goodbye party was last night at the Cheesecake Factory. There were hugs all around, and Anna promised to return for lunch or drinks after work. She entered the office of her young former boss and returned her ID badge and keys to him, wishing him well and thanking him for the lovely photograph of the nighttime view of Boston from the science museum along with her lifetime membership card.

She took a little tour of the Green Wing-back in the public area, smiling at the silently snarling stuffed bobcat and the animals frozen in the vignettes behind the glass enclosures. Then, she crossed the interior bridge that propelled her from Boston to Cambridge in the same building, to the Blue Wing that housed the 4D Theater, the Butterfly Garden, various exhibits, the open lecture stage, and the Theater of Electricity, where flashes of lightning were going off marking the end of a presentation. Anna thought she would see if anyone was around the planetarium, so she rode the escalator back down to the first floor and headed back to the Red Wing.

She passed the large museum store where she resisted the temptation of the gemstone jewelry display from the outside window touching the fire pearls dangling from her ears to remind herself that she did not need new jewelry. She then went past the café, now noisy and filled with nannies done with bringing their charges through the Discovery Center. The multi-colored T-shirted school children were already squeezing into packed lines at the registers where families buying pizza and burgers were trying to wrangle their hungry kiddies.

At the atrium, she was greeted by the loud clanging of the giant Archimedean Excogitation installation, affectionately referred to as the Tinker Toy. It is a convoluted contraption following the path of rolling balls. Beside the massive noisy installation were the musical stairs with children running up and down, creating atonal songs, and contributing to the general din of the atrium. The three small stairs up to the Omni theater and the planetarium led Anna to quiet bliss. The space outside the Planetarium entrance was her favorite place in the museum. Huge backlit displays of the Hubble photographic images glowed in the muted light of the exhibit. On the right wall was the sequence of our place in the universe. First, the earth, our home. Then, our planetary system with the earth revolving in an ellipse around the sun, then the bright cosmic sash of the Milky Way, followed by the swirl of our spiral galaxy, ending with the Hubble image of deep space showing thousands of galaxies. Those images always made her feel all at once very tiny in the scheme of creation and also quite extraordinary.

Anna saw that the morning show had already finished and the afternoon one wasn't scheduled for a while. So, she opened the door to the planetarium just a bit and saw Carl Davis perched on top of the Van der Graff generator - the star machine. He was making a repair to it and glanced around to see Anna. She liked the way the blue light of the planetarium made the tight grey curls of his hair shine a weird electric blue.

"Hey Anna," he said, "I heard that you were leaving today!"

"Yes, I thought I'd try to catch you before the next show." Anna replied.

"I'm getting ready to plan a lecture that's going to take place right here in the planetarium rather than the open Science Central stage." Carl said. "There's more seating here. It adds a little drama. I'm just waiting for my guest lecturer."

Carl climbed down and approached Anna, who had taken a seat in the first row, placing the tote bag with her photos on the floor.

"How would you like to see the fancy new equipment?" Carl said.

"For sure. A private show?"

"You bet."

Carl proceeded to the control panel station, and after a few moments, the planetarium dome lit up with a massive deep starfield.

Anna craned her neck to scan the field, picking out the Big Dipper and Orian's Belt.

"Now watch this." Carl said enticingly.

The starfield sharply shrank to a tiny dot in the center of the dome. That small dot started to grow ever more quickly until the dome was filled with what looked like an enlarged version of the inside of an atom.

Anna felt like she was traveling through the heart of creation. Carl turned on some throbbing rock music as she traveled dizzily through the ever-changing forms. And then there was silence followed by the soft abstract sounds of a Kronos piece. There appeared a massive web across the dome. At each vertex of the infinite web, there was a sparkling jewel.

"Indra's net." Anna whispered.

Carl's voice floated over the empty seats. "Yes, the symbol of interconnectedness. Each jewel endlessly reflects the actions reflected in every other jewel - an ancient mythical representation that fits rather nicely with modern quantum field theory.

"We're writing scripts for this. Carl said, "Maybe we'll do some adult offerings showcasing these more creative images. They are a little outside the educational mission for the kids."

"Well, this is obviously not going to be for the general public." Anna said, glancing back at Carl, whose dark skin glowed in the light of the control booth and made strange shadows on his face.

The dome went back to the deep starfield. Carl made adjustments to the control panel and joined Anna, sitting next to her.

"So, a little more in our mundane little world, what is life in retirement going to look like?" He asked

"Well, actually, I'm going to open a little studio where I can paint and write and do whatever I please whenever I please."

"How fantastic is that!"

"And I have a little public project that I want to do to start a conversation about the Golden Mean. Or Phi."

"Ahh, the Fibonacci Sequence. I thought that Dan Brown already had the subject covered."

"Oh, I'm not getting into all that blood and guts sort of adventure. I want people to notice the spirals in their environment. Maybe develop an interest in math and art at the same time."

"I'll have to come around and see…." Carl said.

The door to the planetarium slowly opened, and a beam of light crossed the darkness of the planetarium.

"Carl, Carl Davis?"

Anna turned to see a slightly built man with a mane of pure white hair enter the path of light.

"And here is my lecturer." Carl said brightly.

As the man approached, Carl said, "Anna, I would like you to meet Professor Michio Kaku."

Anna was not more than a little dazzled to find herself in the presence of the famous physicist, who specialized in string theory, trying to make astounding quantum thoughts understandable through his many popular books.

Professor Kaku, this is my friend Anna, who is abandoning the museum's finance department to start her own studio, where she will be exploring the mysteries of the Fibonacci Sequence.

"Very nice to meet you, Anna." said the professor in a voice so familiar to Anna since her morning news TV show often invited Kaku to make understandable the mysterious advances that science presented to a lay audience.

"Ah, then you will have to explore the world of galaxies, the biggest spirals of them all." Said the famous physicist. Making an arc with his arm tracing the curve of the planetarium ceiling, "The most interesting problem we have to solve is, 'Where is our place in this great cosmic scheme?'

"It is such an honor, Professor Kaku," But I see you have a lot of work to do with Carl, so I will be going.

"The pleasure is mine, and good luck with your art project."

Anna picked up her handbag and the tote bag holding the photos from her office and hugged Carl.

"Send me the date of the lecture. It will be more special now."

She followed the light path from the one open door out of the planetarium and turned to see the two men in deep conversation.

Anna traced her steps back down the long concourse towards the garage, thinking, "What a remarkable place to have spent my days working at an unremarkable job."

She contemplated the days she had spent in lecture halls, having her worldview changed in the span of forty-five minutes by talks from some of the most innovative minds in the world. She would escape the endless numbers that refused to play nicely together on her calculator with a quick trip to the Butterfly Garden to be refreshed by brilliantly colored butterflies landing on her hands. Often, she would take in the latest traveling exhibit, like the current one showcasing the life-size realizations of Leonardo De Vinci's drawings of tanks, bicycles, and machine guns. These things would not come to life for centuries. And a wall-size reproduction of the Vitruvian Man standing with his arms and legs splayed in an X formation, illustrating, yes, the Fibonacci Sequence.

Chapter 13- A Window in Venice

Anna drew up a chair to the window. She threw the panes open and sat elbows on the sill, her jaw nestled in her cupped hands, gazing down at the water taxi stand thirty yards from the front door and then across the Grand Canal to see rising in the morning mist, the islands of Murano and Burano. In the distance, the Austrian Dolomites, a blue band of snow capped mountains.

Paul's snoring as he slept in the bedroom and the lapping of the waves against the taxi platform were the only things that broke the morning silence.

Anna sipped on her strong Italian coffee as she remembered the greeting on the floor of the airport, a marble square with brass lettering that proclaimed, "tutti qui passi che ha fatti nella mia vitta mi hanno per ato qui ora." - "every step I have taken in my life has led me here."

So many steps, tentative, confident, misguided, straight and sure, convoluted and winding, so steep and challenging, leaving one breathless and lightheaded on hard pavement with aching feet and heart, soft steps on grassy and welcoming knolls under sun-drenched skies, cautious mincing, steps in unknown territory and broad strides into unknown adventures. Every step leading Anna here, through some enchantment to Venice.

Walking down the long hall to her studio, Anna saw Karen with a handful of brushes heading towards the common sinks. Anna waved hello, and Karen picked up the pace of her gait to hurry to Anna.

"The empty studio has been finally rented!" Karen breathlessly said.

"Have you met your new neighbor yet?" queried Anna

"Yes, indeed, and an attractive addition he is!"

"Painter, sculptor, artisan, quilt maker?"

"Painter, an oil painter. Very good too."

"I'll have to pop in and check him out."

"You'll be impressed, I assure you. Tea later?"

"You bet! I'm planning on being here for a few hours. Is the Tea Lady in her studio?"

"Yes, see if she has any interesting pastries lying about."

Anna opened her studio door and noticed it could use a little touch-up paint again from open studio traffic damage. She put down her handbag and decided that before she changed into her paint-splattered mules and smock, she'd welcome the newbie just two doors down.

She approached the open door and stopped in her tracks at the delightful vision before her – a Murano glass candy dish loaded with caramel bullseyes sitting on a decorative table whose top surface was made to look like a large paint-splattered palette sitting on three black entwined metal legs.

Without so much as an informal greeting, Anna said, "My favorite! May I?"

Simon Radovich turned away from the easel and said, "Help yourself, I insist."

Anna blushing a bit, said, "Oh, I'm so sorry. I'm Anna Stockton, two doors that way." Pointing in the direction of 512A.

"Welcome to the fabulous 5th floor of Western Avenue Studios." she said.

"Delighted to be here." Simon said with a broad grin as Anna unabashedly helped herself to three bullseyes.

Simon had the good looks of a military man, maybe ten years her junior.

She looked around at the walls of his studio, where he had mounted beautifully framed canvases, all painted with Italian themes in imagery that was bold and clean.

These are gorgeous! Anna exclaimed. Somebody has a great love for Italy.

"I lived there for a while and did some business with the Italians," Simon said, "But I'm retired now. Living the good life."

"What did you retire from?" Anna said, munching candy, drawn to an atypical depiction of gondolas.

"I worked for the government after leaving the Marines. But they're always calling me on special projects because the young kids don't know the old systems."

"Glad to know the government values the wisdom of their elders." confirming in her mind that, yes, he was military.

"Well, I won't take you from your work, but please drop into my studio. My husband's photography studio is right across the hall. I have a feeling you would enjoy his work.

"Nice of you to drop by, Anna. I'm certain I'll be talking to you about how to fit in here."

"I'm fairly new here, too. Everyone has been very welcoming. Thanks for the bullseyes, I thank you, and my dentist thanks you."

"Hah, we're in collusion." Simon said and raised a hand in goodbye.

Paul sat across from Anna at the dining room table, cutting into a thick steak. He had prepared a special extravagant meal of steak and baked potatoes with sour cream and a green salad.

He looked across at Anna and exposed the purpose of such extravagance.

"What city would you choose to celebrate turning seventy in?" Business was good, and Paul wanted to do something special for Anna.

"Seriously?" Anna said, her almond eyes getting large with surprise.

"Seriously." Paul said, thinking certainly it would be his beloved Montreal,

"Venice?" said Anna uncertainly.

"Venice? Why, Venice?" Paul tried not to show that he was somewhat taken aback.

"I've always wanted to go there. St Mark's Square, gondolas, Harry's Bar, lots of things. And they are sinking into the ocean. So I want to see it before it's gone."

"Venice. OK then. I'll do some research and look at flights. It would be a great place to photograph."

Anna's heart leaped a bit at this unexpected conversation. She knew the idea could very well fall by the wayside but determined that she would keep it alive.

****

Simon was saying, "Maybe you know more than you're admitting."

"I know that everything can be made into a symbol. But sometimes a cigar is just a cigar."

Simon smiled at the Freudian reference. "Frankly, I think there's something to it."

Anna had come to Simon's studio searching for caramel bullseyes when the subject of misinterpretation of one's artistic offerings came up.

"I'm not religious. I don't mind that other people are seekers and believers, but that's just not me."

Simon wryly looked at her. "You may be opening some doors you didn't know existed."

"Look, Simon, I know that true believers jump to conclusions when they get a little information about quantum physics and the weird things that happen at a subatomic level. Like how physical laws of space and time become suspended. But we live in a Newtonian world of our senses that make all that space/time continuum stuff solid enough." Anna said.

"It just gives me a headache to try to accommodate people and their insistence on applying their philosophical point of view on a rather simple and lovely idea."

Simon said, "And yet you are driven to continue with the project."

"For now, anyway." Anna said, thinking that she wasn't about to give in the those who willfully contradicted her aims.

Nora had gathered a group of twenty to come to Anna's studio to discuss the Phi project. It started well enough, with Anna giving a short talk on the math behind the symbol. But then it started to become clear that this was just a bit too much like some sort of mini version of a Crystal Cathedral service. A couple of people, with glazed eyes, treated Anna like a pseudoscience prophet. She attempted to bring everyone down to earth, but her capitalistic instincts won out when those gathered purchased prints of her Phi paintings and the collector buttons. She somehow promised that they could meet again, telling herself that would be another opportunity to get the group to see things more clearly.

"But, Simon, "Anna said, desperate to change the subject, "we're going to Bella Italia!"

"You are? That's wonderful! Bravo!" said Simon.

Anna considered Simon's paintings of gondolas. "We're going to see them." She said, putting her into an infinitely better mood.

"How far are you in your plans?' he said.

"Not far, just looking into good places to go and see."

"Have you booked a hotel yet?"

"No, I suppose that should be at the top of the agenda after booking our flights." she said.

"I have an old friend who has an apartment she rents out in Venice. She's not expensive, and it's a nice residential area away from the tourists."

"That sounds wonderful! We could live like typical Venetians going to local bars for lunch and buying brioche to eat at home in the morning, shopping at the nearest frutta & verdure and wine merchant." Anna said dreamily.

Simon promised to look up the information and pass it on to Paul and Anna.

Anna floated back to her studio, fantasizing about living la dolce vita.

****

Paul woke up and came into the kitchen, poured coffee for himself from the funny pot that boiled the water from the bottom section, with the coffee then bubbling up to the top section. He took a brioche from the box lettered with unfamiliar Italian, and got the jar of marmalata from the refrigerator. Enjoying his colazione, he looked at Anna, who turned to him and just pointed to the view with a big grin on her face.

"Not bad, huh? Simon certainly has some nice friends." He said.

Mirella, the owner of the apartment, had met them in the pouring rain the previous night. Taking them up to the second floor, which was called the first floor in this country, she welcomed them and apologized for her limited English. Anna and Paul had worked for weeks trying to master some basic travel Italian, so they managed to communicate enough to understand the rental rules.

"Celestia," Mirella explained as she opened the door to the apartment,"…is a quiet neighborhood. You must stay quiet between 1:00 and 3:00. Everybody is sleeping then. And you must remain quiet after 10:00 PM."

"No wild parties?" Anna said, hoping Mirella had a sense of humor.

"No wild parties!" Mirella said with a smile. She instructed Anna and Paul on how the Italian appliances worked and showed them the list of emergency numbers.

Anna noticed a basket holding pastries, cookies, a pot of jam, and a small packet of coffee.

Mirella gave them directions to the local bar and shops and the grocery store not far away. And making sure they had her phone number nearby, she went on her way, telling them in passing that Celestia was a quiet, safe neighborhood. "No crime, no crime." She said emphatically.

Thanking her, as Mirella left, Anna took one look at the cozy setup and said to Paul, "Can we live here permanently?"

Chapter 14 – Lost in Venice

If you're in Venice, you are lost.

˙That's what Anna heard a local tell a group of Americans who were totally out of their depth trying to negotiate the maze-like streets of Venice. So Anna learned to memorize markers like fountains or an unusual window. Some street names were painted on the walls of the buildings, often worn away by time and weather.

After getting hopelessly lost the first time out, with Paul insisting that he knew the way, only to end up at the same dead-end street facing the same waterway three times, Anna now felt she could find her way to their temporary home with not too much trouble on her own.

They had spent the day touring the city, examining the basilica, and wandering around St. Mark's square, darting down side streets to see what was hidden there. They found numerous bars and gelato stands and high-end shops, Missoni, Chanel, Versace, Armani, Dolce & Gabbana, where Anna only dreamed of shopping. She would stick to the open markets that lined the road along the Grand Canal.

To celebrate the reason why they were there, Anna's turning seventy, they went to a fabulous lifestyle of the rich and famous restaurant called Il Ridotto. There, they indulged in a six-course chef's menu, savoring the nouvelle cuisine placed delicately on each serving platter, each morsel a piece of culinary art.

The staff was surprisingly friendly and accommodating. The server, who looked like a Botticelli angel, explained each course. A young man attended when each course was completed, silently removing the dishes and refilling water and wine glasses. The chef came out to wish Anna "Tanti Auguri," and the stylish hostess wearing big round multicolored eyeglasses approached Anna, leaning down and saying, "Mia madre is celebrating her 70th as well." When a fleet of desserts presented on a pristine white rectangular plate was being offered, the lights went out in the small exclusive restaurant, and the amiable hostess encouraged those seated at the other eight tables to sing "Happy Birthday" in English, with the other well-dressed diners good-naturedly joining in. The hostess presented the dessert plate herself with a dorky little twisted candle lit to illuminate the carefully crafted desserts. The staff came out to say goodbye, and the other diners wished her "Happy Birthday" as they left. Anna felt like a celebrity as she thanked them for their extraordinary grace in making this visit memorable.

"This was definitely superior to the Olive Garden's birthday party experience," Anna said to Paul outside the restaurant. And they joined the night crowd in their passiagiatta.

Anna drank too much Prosecco and was feeling dizzy and full of incredible cuisine. She thought. Italy is such a symphony of in-season foods - freshly made plates of pasta, ragu, anchovy pizza runny with melting cheeses, vongole, Parma ham, freshly caught fish, pecorino in honey, breaded artichokes, gelato, chocolata calda, it goes on and on, one gastronomic heavenly gift after another. Walking around the city seemed the cure for their overindulgence.

Paul wanted to stay behind to continue to take more photos, although he had taken hundreds already. Anna was tired and wanted to have an early bed, so she encouraged Paul to stay and decided to walk back rather than take the water taxi. As she left the busy tourist area, Anna got closer to the quiet sections of regular neighborhoods, away from the crowded centro, breathing in the lingering cooking smells. The night darkened as she made her way, and Anna realized that she had succeeded in getting to Celestia easily on her own. The streets were abandoned, dark, and silent as she made her way. She kept reminding herself that Mirella insisted that there was "no crime, no crime" in Celestia. But as she wandered the tangle of streets, she became uneasy with the shadows and started to imagine footsteps on the cobblestones. She began to think that there was someone close behind her as she turned each corner and wished she had taken the water taxi with the exit so close to the front door. A lone woman burdened with shopping bags came from the direction of the taxi stand passing her.

Anna began to hurry, and when she reached a familiar stone arch, she knew the apartment building was just around the corner. She looked back and saw no one, but still, she broke into a faster pace running a bit as she approached the door and nervously fiddled with the key and, once inside, gave the heavy door a push to make sure that it was locked. Anna ran up the stairs and entered the apartment, and locked the door. She went over to the window and looked out to see someone turning the corner but caught only the sight of a pant cuff and a scuffed shoe. American, she thought. Italians polish their shoes. She went to the opposite window and peered out to see only a young boy quickly making his way along the narrow footpath along the canal that caused him to hold on to the metal prongs piercing the brick wall constructed there, balancing himself expertly as he went.

"You silly, silly woman." she admonished herself and started to hand-wash dishes left in the sink from breakfast, hoping that Paul would return soon.

Chapter 15 – The Doge's Palace

Sheets of rain drove the line waiting to enter the Doge's Palace under the loggia, packed together like anchovies in a tin can. Anna had only one hour to take in the museum before meeting up again with Paul, who had no interest in the dark and gloomy palace.

As the line slowly advanced, Anna shivered not only from the cold blasts of air but the general feeling of a malevolent grandness that the palace exuded. She pulled her rain slicker tighter around her as she roamed the dark rooms and damp stone corridors. From the grand Giant's Staircase and the elegant Ducal lodgings to the rooms full of dark wooden throne-like seats where the aristocracy would determine the fate of the citizenry under enormous paintings depicting the history of their privilege and power. It's hard to imagine, as an American from a country where there is no Golden Book of Aristocratic families, to be allowed to marry only within their class. We do our best to create an aristocracy based on a mere couple of hundred years plus in existence. We promote billionaires, rock stars, and politicians to our top-dog status. It's all comical when you see the lineage represented here. The portraits of the heads of state were still to be observed as modern doppelgangers roaming the streets of Venice outside this stifling atmosphere of social constraints and manipulations of powerful families.

The Bridge of Sighs is anything but romantic from the inside, a narrow corridor of despair heading toward prison, mistreatment, and death. The armory is filled with the heavy, brutal things of war and torture. There are allowed brutalities in the preservation of the most cultivated values.

It's all here, perhaps as written in our DNA. The drive to cultivate and preserve a special breed of humanity above all others. The aristocracy's right to bypass mores and common values when it comes to the treatment of ordinary folks. Anna went into the gift shop and passed by the postcards and glossy art reproduction books. She picked up a deck of playing cards where the kings, queens, and jacks were portraits of Venetian aristocratic figures. There you are, she thought. It was all in the luck of the draw. She wondered if one could ever be free from the mentality of class and desperation to be somehow connected to the chosen few. What things will people do to be among the chosen? And how we create our masters when none are apparent.

The sun was shining when Anna rejoined modern Venetian society outside with the crush of international tourists and the carts selling their colorful goods.

Chapter 16 – Arsenale and Tea

"Take my picture, take my picture!" Anna shouted as she mounted the stairs to the bridge at Arsenale.

Paul did little to make his annoyance clear. He disliked having his attention diverted from "real" photography to take scrapbook pictures.

But he obliged reluctantly, taking his time adjusting the lens.

Standing at the bridge's center, Anna turned to wave to Paul, who stood on the pavement below her. In the distance, where the cafes and kiosks were spread along the canal, she planned her next stop to buy a colorful scarf. Her eyes browsing among the carts filled with refrigerator magnets, T-shirts, and postcards, she seemed to see a familiar face at a distance. She could not be certain.

She smiled for Paul as he took his photos, then ran down the steps and towards the carts, shouting to Paul, "I'll be right back."

As she weaved her way through the carts, resisting the temptation to shop, she approached a cafe that was starting to fill with tourists ready for lunch. She scanned the outdoor tables, and in the back, under an awning, she was taken aback to see Simon Bradovich reading an Italian newspaper and sipping a glass of red wine.

She walked slowly towards him. He glanced up and smiled, waving his hand to acknowledge her.

"Ciao Simon, I didn't know you were going to be in Italy at the same time as we are."

"I was hoping I would run into you two." He said amiably.

"You should have mentioned it." Anna said. "Or were you avoiding us?"

Simon laughed and said, "Not at all. I just wasn't sure that I would be in your neighborhood until my business here was confirmed. Luckily, we wrapped things up quickly, and I'm taking a couple of days to stick around and unwind. Are you enjoying yourselves?"

"It's a dream. Un sogno. I don't want to go home. However, I'm trying to stay out of Paul's way while he's doing his photography. He's been promised a show at Gallery Z of his work from this trip."

"Well, what are your plans for tomorrow?" asked Simon.

"Tagging along with Paul and trying not to break the bank shopping."

"Why don't I treat you to high tea at the Hotel Danieli tomorrow, then? If Paul wants to join us whenever he's done, he's welcome too."

"That sounds wonderful! He'd love to have me out of his way for an hour or two." She jumped up from her seat and said, "Gosh, I need to find him before he thinks I've disappeared."

Simon signaled the waiter and passed him some euros, and said, "Let me help you, and I'll let him know that I'm treating his wife and giving him a break at the same time."

They approached Paul, who was sitting on a bench, adjusting his camera lens. He looked startled as he saw Anna and Simon approaching.

"Simon, I didn't know…."

"A happy coincidence. Good to hear you two are having such a great time. Getting the money shots?"

"Doing my best." Paul said, shaking Simon's hand.

"Simon has offered to take me out of your hair and to tea at the Hotel Danieli tomorrow. It will give you some time to yourself, and you can join us whenever you're done for the day."

Paul was a little reluctant to hand over his wife to a man he did not know well but was tempted to have some time to go at his own pace wherever his interests led him.

"Fine by me, and if I don't have to wear a fancy tea hat, I'll join you when I've had enough for the day."

All agreed, and they went their separate ways, Paul and Anna, to catch a water taxi to prepare a meal in their Celestia apartment. Simon disappeared into the crowd at Arsenale.

****

High tea at the Hotel Danieli, off-season, is quiet and reserved. The plush rooms are decorated in red brocade, and the soft lighting from sparkling chandeliers is flattering as you settle yourself in the comfortable bucket chairs.

Anna spotted Simon sitting on a settee under a classic painting in a heavy gold museum frame. He was sipping on a glass of brandy. She hesitated for a moment, wondering if she should sit across from him in a bucket chair or join him on the settee. Deciding that it would be easier to share sandwiches on the settee, she settled herself against the arm with a comfortable distance between them.

A handsome Italian waiter looking like he was sent from Italian cinema central casting approached them. Simon ordered two glasses of Prosecco and high tea and chatted amiably with the server, who welcomed them to Venice. The attractive young man asked if they found Venice weird.

"It is weird - no wheeled vehicles, except carts. But that's wonderful/weird." Anna said.

The bubbly glasses of Prosecco arrived, accompanied by salty nibbles. Anna loved that most of the time, in this country, you were offered so much more than a small bowl of stale salted peanuts. Instead, drinks were served with olives, crackers, and bits of cheese, usually gratis.

The waiter explained the multiple courses of their tea and asked for their tea choice. Anna and Simon settled on English Breakfast tea. Soon they were presented with current scones with clotted cream and an assortment of jams, an array of tiny sandwiches cut in lovely shapes filled with fish paste and egg salad, pickles and butter, watercress, and Parma ham, and almost too pretty to eat pastries formed like miniature artworks.

Anna felt comfortable with Simon, and the conversation with him was funny, sophisticated, and informative. He was well-traveled and had tales to tell of his adventures. The waiter came to add hot water to their teapot as they consumed the heavenly pastries.

Then Simon leaned close to Anna and said, "Tell me about your street art project. What do you call it? Find the Phi?"

"How nice of you to be curious," Anna said, all the while thinking. "Why would someone so worldly be finding her project anything but mundane?"

But she explained, trying to keep it brief. She was interested in how Leonardo da Vinci and many other artists used the Fibonacci sequence to bring harmony to their artworks. Working at the science museum got her into the conversation about the spiral form's occurrence, created from graphing this elegant mathematical formula in nature, leaving one to think that nature had a preference for harmony and balance. And reading about quantum theory led the uninitiated to make assumptions about these natural forms.

Anna mentioned that she was becoming concerned about Nora and the spirituality she was bringing to the project. Anna only wanted people to hold the idea lightly as a reminder of the beauty in the everyday.

Simon looked so directly at her that she shifted a bit and turned her head away from his gaze. Then, he said almost coldly, "Why did you choose the lower-case Phi? That's not what is associated with mathematics and science."

"Well, I thought it was more graceful. I wanted to use it as a reference to my take on the idea, so I stayed away from the capital Phi. Why does this strike you as so out of the ordinary?"

Simon reached into his jacket pocket and took out a small velvet bag with a gold cord. He untied the cord and dropped the contents of the bag into his hand. It was a small round pin with an all too familiar image. It was a replica of Anna's painting of the Phi image. Only this was rendered in rich blue and polished gold.

"May I?" Anna said and took the pin from Simon's hand. Her almond eyes went wide as she examined the familiar design. Had she seen this symbol before and just not remembered? She had books at home describing symbols.

She examined it under Simon's steady gaze. He seemed to be trying to assess her familiarity with the pin she held gingerly in her palm.

The pin was encased in a circle of gold. It gleamed under the light of the chandeliers of the Danieli; the back of the pin was Lapis Lazuli. When you turned the pin, the front was a thin layer of milky quartz, casting the Lapis Lazuli into a soft blue haze. At the center of the pin was a graceful swirl of gold in the shape of a lower-case Phi.

"What on earth......?" Anna said, breathless, both from the beauty of this rendering of her design and the understanding that there was some confusion about how this rendering came to be.

Simon seemed to relax at the sight of Anna's all-too-obvious consternation. He took the pin from her hand and replaced it into the velvet bag, putting it into the inside pocket of his suit jacket.

"I found it in a shop here." Simon said, "Of course, I immediately thought of you."

"That's quite a coincidence. I mean, you're being here and finding that." Anna pointed to Simon's vest pocket where the bejeweled pin was now hidden from view.

"Let's not mention it again. I don't want you to be unsettled." Simon said.

Anna saw the heavy doors open momentarily, flooding the room with light. Paul entered smiling broadly, plopped into a bucket chair, dropped his assemblage of photo equipment on the floor, grabbed one of Anna's tiny sandwiches, and signaled the waiter to order a brandy.

"Well, he said, smiling, "what have you two been up to?"

Chapter 17 – Flying Home

The last vaporetto ride was bittersweet. Anna kneeled on the seat to take one last look, pronouncing the now-familiar stops along the way. Celestia, Bianalle, Arsenale. She glanced at the hundreds of cafe tables where she wished she was still enjoying espresso and brioche. Squinting in the late afternoon sun, she was sure she spotted Simon having coffee with another man at one of the many tables. The other man turned. It was Rick Berman. Shocked, Anna sunk back into her seat. Thinking the bright lights of the sparkling water must be playing with her imagination. Venice does strange things to one's mind. She stood and watched again, trying to look back to the Arsenale cafe tables, but they had disappeared into the distance.

"I am losing my mind." She thought, "A lot of people have similar looks. I'm ridiculous."

"I will talk to Simon when we get home."

****

"Do you mind if I use your computer access?"

The woman seated next to Anna had been fumbling with the WiFi connection for her assigned seat on the plane returning from Italy.

"I insist!" Anna replied. "I won't be using it at all."

"I need to write while everything is fresh in my mind." The woman was an attractive brunette American of a certain age.

She extended her hand to introduce herself. I'm Melanie.

"Anna." "Are you journaling?"

"So to speak. I just got back from a paid vacation on the Amalfi Coast." Melanie smiled. "I'm a travel writer. I was reviewing a small, charming hotel."

"Oh, may I have your life?" "How was your stay?"

Melanie raised an eyebrow and chuckled, not a little self-satisfied.

"My room was situated high on a cliff with a spectacular view of the ocean. My hosts treated me like family. And the food…well, the food was delicious and beautifully presented."

"Ahhh, I need to read that review and daydream." Anna said.

Where are you coming from? Melanie asked.

"The North. Venice, Verona, Modena – for the Ferrari fan", Anna pointed to Paul, who was already snoring in his seat."

"First time to Italy?"

"No, Paul is a fine arts photographer. He did the Firenze Biennale a couple of years ago. We stayed in Florence for ten days. Lived like locals, met fantastic contemporary artists from all over the world, and snuck away for one day in Rome."

"How wonderful! I come here often. I also write travel guides and arrange tour groups now and then."

Melanie passed her business card to Anna, saying, "I have a book coming out soon. If you have any interest, check out my website."

Anna glanced enviously at the colorful card, representing such an enviable lifestyle.

The two women chatted amiably about family, travel, struggling with trying to speak in Italian, and Italy's joys over glasses of prosecco provided by the flight attendants.

"Well," Anna said wistfully, "I don't want to keep you from your work."

Melanie stretched a bit, stiff from the seat constraints, and said, "Yes, I guess I'd better get at it."

Anna promised she would contact Melanie again through her website. As lunch was served, they shared bits of conversation over the surprisingly edible airplane food, Italian style. Paul jumped in a bit to profess his newfound love for all things Italian.

As the overhead lights lowered and quietly fell over the passengers, Anna wondered what it would be like to be so sure of one's place in life. Melanie had found such a wonderful way to go about her days in mid-life and get paid for what she loved. Paul was obsessed with the geometry of beauty and was so talented in capturing that fascinating, essential magic. They were so fulfilled by what they did with their lives.

Anna felt like a dilettante dabbler, always chasing rainbows. Usually, someone else's rainbows. She was contentedly basking in reflected glory. She was the designated appreciator. She remembered a colleague once saying to her that everyone wanted to be appreciated. She may have wished for that but had no expectations of experiencing such a thing. She was sure that her talent was facilitation. That was a hidden talent. She didn't think she wanted the spotlight. She remembered doing amateur theatrics with her daughter, Audrey, when she was a young girl. The spotlight was hot. You had to be careful that the lighting did not cast unflattering shadows. She wanted to dance and play with the others, but at the periphery of the fun and games. She guessed it was because she was the tag-along kid, always accompanying her two older sisters, closer in age, in their adventures.

Wanting to be seen was such a pathetic and needy ambition. Feminists would say that it was utterly one's own fault if you were not seen. Doubts about the worthiness to be seen were usually at the core of that imposter syndrome. It was frustrating to Anna that she would be caught up in such a common and unnecessary emotion plaguing many women. She took the occasional compliment with grace and no false modesty but somehow always turned the compliment away from herself – "Aren't you so nice to say that."

Why couldn't she admit, "Yes, I am pretty fabulous!"

She looked at successes that had a natural shelf life as ultimate failures. She had nothing to offer as a legacy. And even now, in her last-ditch effort to offer a small piece of herself to the world, there were complications and perhaps even unanticipated dangers. Should she give up? Was it just written in the stars that she would not shimmer and give off light all her own?

Chapter 18 – Complications

Anna made her way to Simon's studio. She was looking for clarification as well as bullseyes. She stopped at his open studio door to see it empty. He was gone. She dashed next door to see Karen as she worked on another pub painting.

"Simon's gone?" Anna asked.

"Yes, he said he was called back to work on some government project. So, he had to close shop. It was quite sudden."

Anna tried to exchange a few pleasantries with Karen, but her brain was spinning with crazy conspiracy theories and fantastic assumptions.

She returned to her studio. "Stop, stop, stop!" she repeated to herself. "This is madness. I am truly losing my mind."

She busied herself with sorting through brushes and paints, trying to order her mind as she put her materials in order. Then, she noticed that a note had been left under her door. From Nora - cheery note welcoming Anna back, saying they had a lot to discuss.

Nora's group was growing out of the space in Anna's studio.   First, there were ten, then twenty coming for regular monthly meetings. When it grew to over 50, Anna had to rent the Onyx Room, the black box theater at WAS. She had to charge a small amount to cover the rental costs. She heard that some of the attendees also met more often in their homes, sometimes weekly.

It was getting out of control. If Anna had a conflict and couldn't make a meeting, Nora would volunteer to lead the group discussion.   Some discussions went far afield from just looking for spirals in one's environment. People were attaching their spin, religious, philosophical, or New Age-y to the Phi symbol to which Anna had given life. Her infant project was now turning into a fractious child and heading towards a rebellious teen.

Anna tried to keep things under control and keep a light-hearted approach, but there would be passionate discussions on using the symbol best. And she found herself being questioned on how to use the symbol for meditation.   Complications just as Rima had foreseen. Anna had designed a T-shirt with the phrase "Find the Phi repeated and stretched into a spiral coil with the Phi symbol at the end. She was starting to see the T-shirt in bars and in stores, tucked under leather jackets and under cozy granny sweaters.

The T-shirt and button sales and contributions more than paid the rent for her studio. If she were to be honest with herself, she was enormously flattered to be the author of something trendy. And it was good to be taking in some income. Admittedly, it wasn't quite the recognition Anna had anticipated. Still, she tried to ride the wave of popularity while it lasted, thinking that people could very well get bored and go on to the next shiny object.

She would repeat the original goal of the project when she went to these meetings. When asked for comment on some particular interpretation, she would always say that wasn't her specific interpretation of the symbol. At the same time, she was very interested in what they had to say. She tried to stay away from magical thinking, all the while acknowledging that some people would have it no other way, displaying a need for some magic and romance in their lives.

Nora would still come by for tea, and she would report to Anna how interest was growing in the Phi project.

When Anna attempted to bring things down to earth, Nora had taken to just giving her a wry look as though Anna was missing the point somehow. Anna did not want to do something that would hinder someone who had done so much to advance Find the Phi.

She also had a fascination with thinking about how a simple idea could multiply like a cell to become a whole new creation. There was something compelling about someone else adding layers to the original work, maybe distorting it, perhaps giving it new life.

She continued to offer the stickers from her studio. She always enjoyed it when a mathematician or a physicist visited, offering their criticisms or admiration for bringing a different take on the symbol to the public.

Anna would take their recommendations on books or scholarly articles. She slogged her way through a book called "Phi" by a famous neuroscientist named Giulio Tononi, who believes the symbol is the seat of consciousness.

She was learning that she had stumbled upon something probably more complicated after her initial first look. More and more, she thought about Indra's net, the ancient story teaching the lessons of connection and reflection. It explained the mechanics of synchronicity.

But she knew that all things also had a natural progression. First, an event, then complexity, then entropy. She started to wait to see the lines of fracture and dissolution and wondered if she would welcome it.

Chapter 19 – Rick's Visit

There was a rare space right in front of the entrance to the studios. Anna pulled in, happy not to have to park as she usually had to at the far end of the lot. It was dusk. Perhaps most of the artists decided to quit early. It wasn't quite 5:00 PM, so the building's front door was still unlocked.

Anna put her studio number magnet on the metal billboard outside the elevator and noticed that there were only a few more left to indicate studios that were open to visitors. She pressed the elevator button, and it arrived quickly, letting out a couple of artists from the 4th floor who greeted her as they squeezed past her trying to negotiate a large canvas that took two to carry.

When she arrived on the 5th floor and started down the wooden halls, she could hear the wooden floors creak beneath her feet in the early evening quiet. One studio was still open across from the elevator doors. She peered in to see the artist putting the final touches on a baseball player's caricature. So close to closing hours to the public, there was no environmental bustle, no music or muted conversation, no laughter. Anna moved along the winding halls, across the hall that bridged two of the old mill buildings admiring new works put out recently on the bridge walls, and reached her deserted building where doors were closed. Apparently, there would be no comradely and gossipy chats to have tonight. She was pleased with this, though. When it was quiet, work time was calm and focused.

Anna entered her studio, switched on the fluorescent lights, checked the water in the coffee maker, and turned it on. She put in a coffee pod and took the cream out of the refrigerator, giving it a sniff that deemed it still fresh, and put her yellow coffee mug in the coffee maker. She watched the coffee drip into the cup, thinking about how nice it was to do something familiar and routine.

She took her coffee and placed it on the work table, and turned to admire the sunset through the old dirty panes giving the rosy and gold colors an impressionist effect. She walked over to the window and started to mix in her mind the paints that could replicate the sunset on canvas. She stood for a while, sipping her hot coffee. Then she turned to see a man standing at the door.

Startled, she spilled a bit of her coffee and, reaching for a paper towel from her work table, stooped to clean the spill from the floor. Gazing up at the man, she said, "Mr. Berman, isn't it?"

"Rick, please. And I'm sorry if I startled you."

"No, please don't apologize," Anna said. "Have a seat. I thought the front door would be locked by now. So, it's lucky you got in. What can I do for you today?"

Anna lifted her mug and said, "Coffee?"

"No coffee, thanks. And I apologize for coming so late in the day without an appointment." Rick said,

"No appointment necessary. Really." Anna said as she gestured towards a nearby stool. Please, have a seat and let me know what prompted your visit?" Anna smiled as brightly as she could, but her mind was racing, recalling the conversation with Simon at the Hotel Danieli and the unsure memory of Simon seated at a table with the man standing before her. He pushed the stool closer to Anna and took a seat, folding his hands in his lap. Anna sat in her work chair and glanced at her art tool, brushes, paints, and pencils taking note of a pair of scissors."

"I wanted to talk to you about your "Find the Phi" project. Rick said with a slightly ironic smile.

"Yes," Anna replied, "I saw that you took an interest in all the project materials. Are you enjoying participating in the project? Do you have any questions?"

"As a matter of fact, I do." Said Rick, his smile fading.

"You see, your project is not at all original. No, not at all. And I'm wondering how you came to create it?"

119

"Oh, gosh! Then this about some sort of licensing or royalty thing that I was unaware of?" Said Anna, shifting in her seat uncomfortably. "You must tell me where I went awry here. I thought that this was such a brilliant, original idea." She said, attempting to interject some charm and lightness into her smile.

"Do you mean to tell me that you have never seen this before?" Rick said, reaching into his pocket and opening his hand to reveal the gemstone and gold Phi symbol, the gold encasement glittering in the fluorescent light. The same pin that Simon had shown her at the Hotel Danieli.

"I think I may have seen you in Italy with a mutual acquaintance. Am I correct? It's all so coincidental. I think that this is something that concerns you. If I have committed any sort of transgression to a project of yours, it was not an attempt at plagiarizing. You really must tell me about your concerns." Anna said,

"You probably have learned, through our mutual acquaintance, that this is a symbol of a private organization. Of course, yours is not a replica, but close enough to cause us concern. "

Rick leaned over and put his face closer to Anna's, and said in a stage whisper, "There are people of importance, people of means and power, who comprise this group."

Anna reminded herself of the location of her scissors and took a breath to steady her nerves.

"What does this symbol mean to you and your friends?" she said.

"And why does this seem to cause you such concern?"

"There is much that you don't see, don't understand, can't understand," Rick said. "I need to know what you think you do understand. We need to control this knowledge. There is so much damage that may occur if it is not controlled."

"Thousands of people attend countless seminars, go to ashrams, read the latest Deepak Chopra, and read countless volumes trying to explain the basics of quantum mechanics to the uninitiated, who spend hours looking at YouTube videos touting theories from the ridiculous to the sublime-channeled information from alien entities, world-famous scientists trying to make the ineffable understandable to the general public—meanwhile arguing among themselves as the best and most accurate theories to present, which according to the latest scientific inquiries in this age of impossibly fast information generation, changes daily, if not hourly. You, with your simple little public art project, have hit upon an idea that makes the ineffable somehow accessible because you use symbology instead of the limitations of language."

"To be honest, you may very well fade away like dust in the wind, or you may awaken something that we frankly can't yet define.

And we don't like surprises. So perhaps discretion is the better part of valor. We understand that it may be too late. The seed is planted."

"And who exactly are WE," Anna said nervously.

"We are the descendants of the aristocracy. We are the natural rulers of men. Educated and tempered by centuries of power and wealth." Rick said. "We tolerate the outward appearance of democracy, but that, after all, is such a messy, unpredictable, and unworkable concept. Isn't it? So we don't really appreciate interference."

Anna's thoughts went back to the dark Doge's Palace, where generations fought for control of power and wealth among themselves. Centuries of unending conflict.

"Are you threatening me?" Anna asked, trying to hide her trepidation.

"No, Rick ruefully smiled in reply, "because we don't know if some force has been unleashed and who and how any effects will occur and to whom. Including our organization."

"You have a nice life, an agreeable husband, friends, travel, and lively interests. Why would you risk altering that for the unknown? If you take that path, you take us with you. We are not necessarily willing"

"Confusion has been effective so far by widespread misinterpretations spread by media and governments, but if these illuminated thoughts generally become apparent at a subtle level, politically, economically, and spiritually, change will result. It could be most disruptive. For everyone, for you. Are you ready to be made uncomfortable?"

Anna sat back, examining Rick's face.

"I guess when they say that knowledge is power, they don't consider what that kind of power means. We can do much with a disinformation campaign. But we would rather not trouble ourselves." Rick said.

 Anna was quiet, eyes downcast.

Then she looked up to see Rick staring intently at her.

"Then you understand." he said.

"I do." Anna said with an air of inevitability, and a swift shake of her head, sad more than fearful of the unknown, sadness at an opportunity missed, and adventure declined. Her eyes fell to her hands, folded helplessly in her lap. And, unfortunately, a curiosity about what information exactly was being protected.

Rick Berman stood and said, "Very well, then."

Chapter 20 – Conclusions

Anna examined Rick's face as he was speaking. He was so focused on impressing her with the seriousness of his message, the gravity of the subject she had fallen so casually into with her little public art project.

They fell into silence while she absorbed what Rick had said. She glanced down at her folded hands and then examined his face. He had been waiting to see if what he had said had sunk in, looking satisfied that he had hit his mark, and then his gaze shifted as he contemplated Anna.

Anna wondered if he had ever heard of the internet. So many conspiracies and so little time. As he had been talking, she felt like she was taking a trip down memory lane, pausing at all her philosophical locations along the way. She had started as a devout Catholic in the days of Latin liturgy, the pomp, and the ceremony of high masses with glorious music. To this day, she experiences a feeling of sacredness when she hears a classical performance of liturgical music at Symphony Hall or visits one of the magnificent cathedrals and basilicas of Europe. But somewhere in her teens, she arrived at this notion that there was something she was missing, some piece of sacred information that she would like to find. Slowly she abandoned the dogma of the church and studied other beliefs, traditional and occult. She always found the search interesting and flawed in some way or another. She came to understand that she had limited interest in rituals, fascinating though they may be. She came to think of dogma and ritual as tools to reach some psychic understanding that was probably very simple. She liked that the Dalai Lama seemed to need only the commandment of compassion. She thought it could be as simple as the little alien in E.T. gave the simplest of doctrines when he extended his glowing digit and said in his weird voice, "Be Good."

Then there was watching Rima developing her psychic talents over decades. Those days in the '70s and 80s with New Age teachers with their otherworldly guides offering all sorts of alternative realities to consider. Too many who felt they had the answers to live a life above the fray ended up experiencing more than their share of challenges, seemingly to say that when you say you have the solution for humanity, new problems will present themselves to be solved. All the while, be confounded by miraculous cures that could not consistently be repeated and creating events that could not be duplicated, like some cosmic joke on our hubris. But for the most part, it gave an alternative place for people of goodwill to practice compassion and work out a

125

need for rituals and rules. Paganism gave people a structure to respect the earth and be good stewards of their environment.

The Aliens question had become so convoluted and so obviously colored by an individual's philosophical leanings that Anna just wished that if there were other life forms, they would just get over an aversion to such an unevolved society as ours and come along and say hi and have a cup of tea.

So, Rick's story of collusion among the priveledged and powerful was no news and very likely had some amount of truthfulness to it. However, it did frustrate Anna that there seemed to be nothing to be done to combat such forces that have existed for a long time. If the general public remained fascinated and cowed by the accoutrements of status, aristocracy, wealth, and power, the powerful would continue to be the influencers of our evolution. They depend on authoritarianism and religiosity.   And humankind is not apt to give up easily their comfortable social leanings. If there is not an aristocratic structure in place, we will invent one.

Anna's years exposed to science and physics introduced her to the structure of life and the contemplation of what consciousness was, with most scientists skirting around the suggestion that consciousness indeed suggested a godly concept—thinking about the subatomic world where time and space do not exist. Nevertheless, attention seems to be the definer of what will become matter, sending people into all sorts of philosophical puzzles. Everyone is looking for certainty. Everyone is looking for the correct defining theory.

At 70, with all those intellectual and experiential quests behind her, Anna had become comfortable with this her manifesto:

We are all products of DNA, our environment, our historical moments, and our experiences. To move beyond these things may be necessary for our evolution, but it is not always easy or, for some, not even desirable. In his work on mythology, to paraphrase what Joseph Campbell used to say, don't take anyone's mythology away from them or suffer the consequences.

But yes, there is more to life than our day-to-day experiences and beliefs. Too many philosophers, too many poets, too many ancient cultures, and too many others have known and written of a broader life beyond the banal.

But what has that got to do with the price of tomatoes? It indeed comes down to the everyday experiences, how we work, whom we love, how we amuse ourselves, and make our mark in the world. It has nothing to do with a level of ambition until we try to make ambition the law of the land.

So why not create a civil society where all levels of ambition can reside?

Anna considered herself not the kind of person to make any dramatic difference. But she could just give stickers away and remind people that harmony was a mathematical formula that existed all around us and in us—a small way to get people to pay attention.

She spoke to break the silence between them.

"Look, Rick," she said, "I'm not responsible for anyone's dopamine spike."

"I'm not looking to change the world, be anyone's guru, or change anyone's beliefs. I couldn't do that if I tried."

"I'm not proselytizing. And I would rather not people use my images to proselytize. But I see now that I can't stop that from happening. It is within our nature, as they say, to connect the dots."

"And here's the problem with connecting the dots. There is no such thing. Because there is no such thing as a straight line of events leading to a certain conclusion, when you dig down, you will see stops, gaps, and misconceptions all along the way to any conclusion. Scientists do double and triple-blind experiments because they know that they will personally influence results. To me, there is nothing but randomness and patterns. The science you use to justify any organization trying to rule the world is missing one grand thing that we all experience every day. Entropy. Not just the eventual breaking down of things, but if you look much deeper at the tiniest level, there seems to be a tendency towards survival, not so much of the fittest but the most efficient, oddly seeming to favor altruism. Let's face it. Look at all the energy it takes to maintain selfishness. And look at the energy it takes to sit on a blanket in a grassy field on a sunny day and share a sandwich and a glass of wine with someone. The world you live in is fighting for survival for certain. The funny thing is, all you have to do is stop it. But to stop, it would be death to everything you believe in, and you would believe that to be your death. You. Just. Can't."

"So, I'm no threat to you. I don't have the Big Answer to The Big Question. All I ask people to do is to pay attention. Pay attention to beauty and harmony and acknowledge it as pervasive and personal. That's all. I don't have the solution to anyone's problems, and I can't find your soulmate or help you win the lottery or become rich and famous."

"This is what I believe today. With more information, I will feel differently tomorrow. My only real religion is to aim for compassion and kindness and to stay curious."

"I'm small potatoes in the scheme of things, and in time my little project will just fade into insignificance when a more interesting idea comes along."

"We are storytellers. You tell your story, and I will tell mine."

Rick leaned away and examined Anna. She could see him visibly trying to make a connection that would place Anna in some proper role in the scheme he knew to be the truth. But to him, Anna was a loose cannon. She had no real commitment and, therefore, would never be able to grasp the necessity of control. Anna was right about this being about children playing with stickers and thinking pretty thoughts. She was, in fact, insignificant.

He stood up and looked into Anna's eyes, and said, "We have nothing more to say, then. And you do have a valuable protector on your side."

"And one more saving grace. You do have lineage on your side, as well."

Anna tried to control the small gasp that was forming in her mouth. The memory of Audrey's birth came rushing back to her. She was told by her ex-husband's stern uncle that there was a group of people in Scotland awaiting the news of the possible male child to be born to continue the last of a strain of descendants from William the Conqueror.

When it was discovered there was to be a girl child, all conversation and interest ceased. Anna thought it was all nonsense. Everyone claimed some sort of royal heritage. But why did Simon take such an interest in her from the very start?

Anna thought of Simon, smiled, and said, "You already have the stickers. I'm afraid that's all I can provide for you."

Rick stopped at the door and turned at her, and lowered his eyes, and he said, "We never had this conversation."

"What conversation?" Anna replied.

Rick took one last long look at her, then turned, and Anna could hear his steps treading the hall's length.

She locked the door to her studio, put her scissors in her pocket, and decided to take the back hall fire exit to her car.

Chapter 21 – Begin Again

Anna sat across from Nora, who was clearly distraught.

"I'm done, Nora. I'm retiring, closing my studio, and leaving the city. We're done. This project took a direction I never intended. But it remains my project, not yours. You will no longer use my materials. You have no permission to reference me in any way."

"But the work…" Nora said tearfully.

"This was meant to be an individual journey, Nora. Not just another private club or another pseudo-religion. There are many gurus out there who would welcome your enthusiasm. Just. Not. Me."

"I was not trying to create a movement. I was only trying to get you to pay attention. But if you insist on a movement, then understand that its nature will be to move. Move past your assumptions and convictions, and biases. There is more."

"Move past the insatiable need for accumulation and validation through sex, status, sensations, stilettos, anything that diverts the attention from the one rule that will save us. That one rule – Pay Attention. To harmony, to balance, to beauty. You don't have to say a thing. You don't have to form an opinion. Just let the moment resound in the very form that makes you a carrier of the beautiful design of the universe".

Nora's face portrayed a combination of disbelief and anger. Anna gently placed her hands on Nora's shoulders.

"Be kind to yourself. We are all learning. We will get this right if we look for reminders of our power to know what is really essential."

The great biologist E. O. Wilson said that we are creatures with stone-age instincts trying to function in the God-like technological universe we have created."

She could see that the only thing landing in Nora's consciousness was loss and grief. The conversation would just become less and less useful.

She offered Nora a comforting hug and wished her well, gently guiding her to the door.

Nora looked at Anna and shook her head. "Anna, it's too late." she said and walked away, glancing back with her wry smile.

"That done." Anna thought. Now back to the future.

She cleared the last of the cartons from the studio, taking one last look around, enjoying the sunset one last time. She dropped off her keys at Marc's office and chatted with him about future plans. Then she took the dolly with the last of her studio supplies and loaded the cartons into the trunk of her car.

She returned the dolly to the loading dock and took down the magnet, signaling that her studio was open with not a slight feeling of nostalgia for another dream done.

Anna got into her car, turned the ignition, turned on the music - Dimash Qudaibergen's "Across Endless Dimensions," and turned out of the parking lot, looking back at the massive building housing hundreds of studios filled with dreamers. The music soared – "Take me home, back to my soul, give me gold wings so I can touch the sky." ending with Dimash's alien call to the universe.

'I'm going to Louisville and living the carefree life of a retired Southern belle. I will have Linda make me the most spectacular hat for the Kentucky Derby. I'll drink Bourbon and dance in the streets to blues and bluegrass when the bands come in for the summer street festivals. I will wander the galleries in NULU and stuff myself with Cuban sandwiches, and do the pub crawl on weekends in the Highlands district. I'll join my family, the only ones cheering on the Celtics and enjoying hot wings and beer watching sports on the big screens at Roosters. I'll have extra pecans on my Graeter's hot fudge sundae and walk off the calories on the endless beautiful trails in the Parklands. My friends will come to visit, and I will show them what Southern charm looks like. I will leave all of this nonsense behind me. I'm done.'

Anna drove down the long drive and glanced back at the studios in her rearview mirror. She approached the end of the drive, stopped, and put on her right blinker to turn onto School Street. She turned her head to check for oncoming traffic and noticed the back of the Stop sign on the left side of the street. It was covered with tags from artists from the studios. The very bottom of the street sign that was battered and curled up slightly to point to her Phi sticker, which seemed to glow a bit against the sunset sky.

"And then again," she thought, smiling her Mona Lisa smile, "Perhaps, I've only just begun."

The End

Coda

Robert Frost wrote, "We dance round in a circle and suppose, but the secret sits in the middle and knows."

Life will lead the way if you give it a chance. Pay attention.

****

Play with Anna Stockton on You Tube

Moulettes - Patterns

https://www.youtube.com/watch?v=U0Q8k1nhDrU

Dimash - Across Endless Dimensions

https://www.youtube.com/watch?v=B-AShDu7L6A

Indra's Net - The Illusion of Separateness

https://www.youtube.com/watch?v=yD9og3ylAzg&list=TLPQMjcwODIwMjL

The Fibonacci Sequence

https://www.youtube.com/watch?v=2tv6Ej6JVho

136

****

If you would like to participate in Anna Stockton's Find the Phi Project, and receive Phi stickers please contact Anna at info@frindthephi.com.

Acknowledgments

I would like to thank all the fine folks and friends at the Museum of Science, Boston, MA, for the daily exposure to their exemplary work in the sciences and all those who supported their endeavors. I would also like to acknowledge the many lovely artists and art enthusiasts that I have encountered and worked with over the years as an artist, art supporter, and gallerist at Chimera Gallery, Western Avenue Studios, Gallery Z, The Mellwood Art Center, and the fabulous art communities of Nashua NH, Lowell MA, and Louisville KY. All of you have inspired me with invaluable lessons in art and life that I will always treasure.

Thanks to Michio Kaku for making science understandable to the uninitiated. And thanks to the Moulettes, who make science a matter of music, and Dimash Quedaibergen, who makes music matter.

Thanks to my extraordinary daughter Jennifer and my beautiful granddaughters for contributing to my characters and, of course, Sonny, who provided the opening of my novella. And thanks to Art's talented family for helping to understand Everything.

My girlfriends are a constant source of support and inspiration, so thanks to Judy and Susan C,
Susan D, Karen, and the magical Carole.

Finally, I want to thank my amazing fine arts photographer husband, Art (yes, I am married to Art), for memorable travel adventures and explorations in all manner of art and ideas that have enriched my life with days I once only dreamed possible.

About the Author

Nancy Ferrier studied art at the Cape Conservatory in Barnstable, MA, and was the director of Chimera Gallery in Nashua, NH, from 2006 to 2011, which was dedicated to presenting works of emerging contemporary artists.

She then opened her own studio in Western Avenue Studios in Lowell, MA, where she created an interactive street arts project called Find the Phi.

She also worked at the Museum of Science in Boston, MA, in Finance for 23 years, where she was able to immerse herself in all manner of lectures and science information and had the good fortune to meet many luminaries involved with science.

Upon retiring, she wrapped her Find the Phi project in an interactive novella entitled Anna Stockton's Theory of Everything.

She now resides in Louisville, KY.

www.ingramcontent.com/pod-product-compliance
Lightning Source LLC
Chambersburg PA
CBHW070645220526
45466CB00001B/298